COINCIDENCE
OR
THE HAND OF
GOD?

May Jesus our
Lord & Savior help
you get past whatever
that is holding
it is you back.
Blessings,
Cewl

COINCIDENCE
OR
THE HAND OF GOD?

Cindy Hess Elks

ACKNOWLEDGMENTS

To my dearest sisters in Christ, Reverend Carmen Warner Robbins, Lynn Bailey, and Gwen Hurst, who gave so much time, love, and prayers to help my family and me break free of the curses, vows, and grasp of Satan. You were so diligent in supporting me; plus, through the years of our friendship, you've helped me understand the wholeness of the Bible.

I also owe my life and gratitude to the Bandals, Pastor Norma Guerrant, Mary O'Benedict, Olivia Roscamp, Mary Schmidt, Pastor Mary Lou Flesh, Pastor Don Crary, Dana Erwin, Cathy McLean, and others, for their commitment to pray for me to be set free of the bonds of depression, hatred, and revenge. Many times, I was too doubtful, too weary, too depressed to even talk to God. But all of you went to war for me.

To David Flesh, Lea Schoenwetter, Mark and Phyllis Jennings, Libby Palm, and Tom O'Neill, each one of you gave so much time and energy in editing this manuscript for publication. I love you all so very much.

Finally, sweet Jesus, you granted me the gift of freedom from the crushing burdens of depression and hatred and opened my heart to receive your healing love and forgiveness.

TABLE OF CONTENTS

Foreword 9

Preface 11

Introduction 13

My History—1955 to 2021 17

Vision One: The Fort 23

Vision Two: The Crevice 33

Vision Three: The Peppercorn Seed 47

Vision Four: My Stepmother and the Demon 57

Vision Five: Mom, a Belt, and the Hand 67

Vision Six: The Tar Pit 73

Vision Seven: Beaten by My Dad 81

Vision Eight: The Dingy and the Wire 91

Vision Nine: The House and the Rocks 99

Vision Ten: The Kid on the Roof 109

Vision Eleven: New House, Rooms, and Communion . .123

The Miracle of a New Job 135

The Miracle of the Mysterious Book 147

The Miracle on the Road 153

The Miracle of the Shootings .159

Epilogue 171

References 177

FOREWORD

What do we do when the path before us is dark, the instructions given are wrong, or the destination is unclear?

Each of us encounters times in our lives when our next step is uncertain. In Cindy's own journey laid out in these pages, I see three moments when she was called by God to:

- begin right where she was in that moment;
- use what she had within her, in that moment; and
- do what she could, in that moment.

This book will touch you personally in your own journey. As Cindy shares with you her own experiences when faced with challenges and adversity in life, you may be able to relate to your own struggles.

- God *reaches* each one of us just where we are;
- God *invites* us to use the circumstance that He has allowed; and
- God *empowers* us to overcome and reach peace.

Through the compassionate love of Jesus, may your journey rise above coincidence to be one that is led by the Hand of God.

—Reverend Carmen Warner-Robbins

September 2021

PREFACE

Have you ever wondered what is behind light and darkness in the world? Why is there good and bad all around us? Why do some claim a miracle has happened? Are they misled? I don't think so.

Sometimes things go so well in this life. But then there are times when everything is coming out of the dark voids in the earth and blocking us on our path.

What is it about choices in life? Do we go up, do we go down, do we go to the left, do we go to the right, do we do good, or do we do bad? What is it that helps us make our choices?

Are there forces behind the scenes in life? Join me on my journey and see what I have learned about light and darkness in this world, why there are good and bad situations, some of the unseen forces that are helping or hindering us, and the significant choices we all must make. You'll never be the same!

INTRODUCTION

If you think God and Satan do not exist, think again! If you think lifelong battles with depression, hatred, un-forgiveness, and revenge cannot be removed from your heart, think again, I'm here to tell you it is possible. I do believe what has happened to me is a gift, not only meant for me but also for all those who will listen to my story. Have you ever driven a car right into the sunset and were unable to see what was ahead? Just because you couldn't see anything doesn't mean there weren't people, cars, a stop sign, or a red light. The same is true when during the light of day, you are surrounded by powers of darkness; there is always something there you cannot see. Through my journey, our Lord Jesus Christ rescued me in the most amazing way at the eleventh hour of my plans to commit suicide.

Part of my hope is to inform people who do not believe in the demonic that they are either *misinformed* or *uninformed*. There are demons that are constantly trying to divert us away from our Heavenly Father. Although Jesus has won the war over hell and death, small battles are still going on. The battle continues here on earth between God and Satan for each one of us. Billy Graham says, "In his warfare against God, Satan uses humanity, which God created and loved. So, God's forces of good and Satan's forces of evil have been engaged in a deadly conflict from the dawn of our history....Satan and his demons are known by the discord they promote, the wars they start, the hatred they engender, the murders they initiate, the opposition to God and His commandments. They are dedicated to the spirit of destruction."

I want to convey to people everywhere that we must make a choice concerning whom we shall follow. It is God's will for all of us to receive eternal life in heaven with unending joy, love, peace, happiness, health, and wholeness, and not to perish. Jeremiah says,

> 'For I know the plans that I have for you,' declares the LORD, 'plans for prosperity and not for disaster, to give you a future and a hope. Then you will call upon Me and come and pray to Me, and I will listen to you. And you will seek Me and find *Me* when you search for Me with all your heart.
>
> Jeremiah 29:11–13 (NASB)

I would not be alive today if it were not for Jesus Christ because He provided a rescue for me from my past. I still find myself tearing up when I think about this fact: *God spared my life, but why?* I know this book holds some of the answers. The God of the Bible still speaks; He still enters our world and touches lives. But most importantly, He comes to do what we cannot do for ourselves. Psalm 34:18 (NIV) says: "The LORD is close to the brokenhearted and saves those who are crushed in spirit."

I pray that you will be encouraged today because no matter what is happening in your life right now, you have a door to a fresh new life and a different future waiting for you. God has never given up on you, no matter what you have done! He is pursuing you. Just "*stop*" in your tracks, quiet the noise in your head, be still and listen for His voice. It says in Romans,

> No, in all these things we are more than conquerors through him who loved us. For I am convinced that neither death nor life, neither angels nor demons, neither the present nor the future, nor any powers, neither height nor depth, nor anything else in all creation, will be able to separate us from the love of God that is in Christ Jesus our Lord.
>
> Romans 8:37–39 (NIV)

He does not want religiosity, but He wants a *relationship* with each of us! There is no sickness, disappointment, person, or challenge too difficult that can keep you from the healing love of God, *except you.* The saying "let go and let God" has a lot of truth in it. *You cannot have what you will not accept!* Turn your hands over and let go of whatever you are holding. Jesus loves us with the kind of love that refuses to give up! The choice is yours. *I say again; the choice is yours.* Satan made his choice, and because he cannot have God's love, he doesn't want us to have it either. John 10:10 (NKJV) says: "The thief (Satan) does not come *except* to steal, and to kill, and to destroy. I (Jesus) have come that they may have life, and that they may have *it* more abundantly." Please pick a side. **Not picking—is picking!**

Some fifty years ago, when I started to fight my battles with depression and anger, I did not have much faith or belief in either God or Satan. *Now, however, my life reflects a major victory and an entirely different story concerning both God and Satan.* I truly believe the same can happen to others.

In the love of Jesus and mine.

Blessings,

Cindy Hess Elks

July 2021

MY HISTORY— 1955 TO 2021

I think my story of how the Lord worked in my life will prove that indeed He did! The main people I'll be sharing about are Jesus, myself, good and bad angels, some family members, and the dear Christian warriors who went into battle for me beginning in 1991. My story is about how God answered their prayers for my family and me and the dramatic God-given visions that I experienced over several years. All these visions happened during very intense prayer times. The first of these visions happened while I was attending a church retreat in an old, rundown meeting hall in the southern California Mountains. I was attending because I desperately wanted to make peace with God, if He existed, before following through on my plans to commit suicide.

My story has a number of life-saving truths that I know others need to hear. These are written down with a heart full of love and hope for those who read this story. Every vision I share with you is truthful and thoughtfully written down as I experienced it. The title of this book, *Coincidence or the Hand of God*, is a question that you'll need to answer for yourself after reading this book. But I think you will agree as you finish reading it that this book came to fruition by the hand of God and through no coincidence at all!

In this book, I will share details of my life, a life that was full of hatred, rage, and "un-forgiveness." The negative emotions that I experienced throughout my life led me to make plans to murder my parents and then commit suicide. But before I could follow through on these plans, I was stopped and radically changed, transformed by the grace and mercy of God's hands. I was uncharacteristically changed to someone who could give love and support to others and witness God's word to people, to the same people that I had wanted to murder. As you read this story, you will understand that it is only by the hand of God that this change happened. Because the deep roots of hatred and "un-forgiveness" had entwined around my heart and mind, it took several years to fully untangle them. And when it was done, I was set free to show God's love, compassion, and tenderness to others.

As a young girl, I suffered beatings, verbal and physical abuse, hunger, neglect, sexual abuse, lies and was made the scapegoat of my family. My undeserved and unwarranted beatings left emotional and physical marks. The neglect toward me in my teens included being forced to live in an unfinished garage where the temperatures ranged from twenty-nine to 105 degrees. I was kidnapped twice, and I was never allowed into the house after I was fifteen years old.

At fifteen years of age, I was forced to get a job to support myself and to pay for all my needs, including food, school, car, insurance, clothes, and medicines, while I was still in full-time school and athletics. I was basically an unwanted child who turned to perfectionism to try to get the tiniest sign of love or acceptance. I went to church and attended a Bible study, never used drugs, never smoked, won numerous awards, and was never promiscuous. Because the neglect and lies from my parents continued for several decades, I eventually reached a point of depression and rage that was unbearable; murder and suicide were my way out of it all.

One spring week in 1987, my brother and I were expected to clean up our older sister's apartment. The apartment was a mess; my only sister had committed suicide by shooting herself in the head with a pistol. Because it had taken the police two weeks to locate next of kin, the smell in her apartment was sickening. Maggots were feasting on her blood, and upon seeing this, I had to rush into the bathroom to vomit. For years I was left with feelings of guilt at not helping her somehow or in some way.

Two years later, after my sister's suicide, my ten-year marriage to an alcoholic ended, deepening my depression. Because of my emotional state and suicidal desires, my psychiatrist sent me to an inpatient treatment facility in another state for therapy and medical treatment. After a month there, my depression deepened even more, and I was transferred to a hospital in another city, where I was put on suicide watch. At this facility, I experienced more drug therapies, private and group therapy, and eventually electroshock therapy, which severely damaged my cognitive abilities. When I was discharged, I unknowingly experienced God's hand as He helped me figure out how to drive my car again and use a map to get home to California. Miraculously I arrived home in one piece, though to this day, I have no memory of the drive.

While I did experience a measure of relief through the many treatments that I received, not one alone was enough to lift the overwhelming burden of depression from my shoulders. After a year, the brain numbness from the shock treatments finally wore off, but I still felt only hatred for my parents, my abusers, and basically for mankind. I felt hopeless and made plans to shoot myself and be done with the torment that I was living in. I got my affairs in order, wrote notes, and mailed them, and then I put my beloved animals to sleep. Next, I decided to attend one more church retreat to make some kind of peace with God, if there was one before I ended my life. I felt in my heart that I had worked extremely hard to beat my depression, using every option that mankind had to offer for more than ten years. But nothing had really worked, and I was at my wit's end, I was ready to succumb and give up the fight for survival, but God had a different plan! He reached down to save me, just as He waits to save each one of us if we only turn to Him. As you continue to read this book, I think you'll agree with me it was by the hand of God that I'm here writing this. May God bless all who read this book!

"Call to Me, and I will answer you, and show you great and mighty things, which you do not know" (Jeremiah 33:3, NKJV).

"For he has rescued us from the dominion of darkness and brought us into the kingdom of the Son he loves, in whom we have redemption, the forgiveness of sins" (Colossians 1:13–14, NIV)

"He (God) heals the brokenhearted and binds up their wounds" (Psalm 147:3, NIV).

"Even to your old age and gray hairs I am he; I am he who will sustain you. I have made you and I will carry you; I will sustain you and I will rescue you" (Isaiah 46:4, NIV).

"I pray that the eyes of your heart may be enlightened in order that you may know the hope to which he has called you, the riches of his glorious inheritance in his holy people" (Ephesians 1:18, NIV).

Comment: I pray that you will understand the incredible greatness of God's power for anyone who believes in Him. He is far above any ruler or authority or power or leader or anything else, not only in this world but also in the world to come.

Father, we come as stumbling, blind children who cannot traverse this world. Lord, out of the goodness of your love, in mercy turn toward us, do not hide your light from us. When we are in trouble and are separated from you, please come near and rescue us. God, we do not fully understand this life or the next nor know how to pray. Send your Holy Spirit to help and intercede for us, we pray.

VISION ONE: THE FORT

All Need to Choose—My Choice

When I was sixteen years old, I accepted Jesus as my Lord and Savior at a high school revival, but soon afterward, battles with depression took over my life. Fast forward to 1991, my now twenty-year struggle with depression was still present even though for the last ten years, I had worked through multiple therapies to beat the depression. None had worked, and this left me with no more inner fight. I had no hope in God, and I was deeply suicidal. My emotional pain was so intense that I felt as if I had soaked myself in gasoline and set myself on fire. One part of my mind wanted to die and end this emotional pain, but another tiny part of my soul still wanted to live. The battleground between these two emotions was horrific. I could hardly think, move, or even breathe.

My Emotional Storm

With a great effort, before I was to commit suicide, I decided to go to a church retreat in October of 1992 up in the mountains to make peace with God, if He existed. But while I was there, I experienced my first vision or impartation (an understanding of the kingdom of God). When I arrived at the old church retreat center, which was over an hour's drive into the mountains east of San Diego, my critical perfectionist spirit kicked in, and my first thought was: why does a church retreat center let its buildings get so worn down? I had been here once or twice before and saw that some of the sixty-year-old cabins had holes in the walls where mice could enter. Most of them had cobwebs inside and out. The furniture was old and very simple. The showers were a mess. The water coming out of the faucets was orange from the rust and iron in the well water. The inside of the toilets was orange in color too. The chairs in the main hall were the old, tan fold-up chairs, which definitely had seen better days. The windows were dirty and just filled the place with gloom. I really didn't enjoy being at this place, but it was a place where I could get away from the phone, television, and the house. I've always felt closer to the Creator out in the woods than I did in my living room.

I arrived late Friday and settled in. On Saturday, the main events took place. I did not want to talk to anyone, so I did not get myself involved with any activities. I sat down in one of the uncomfortable folding chairs towards the back of the hall. I needed some quiet time to make peace with God or whoever was controlling life before I drove home on Sunday, got my rifle on Monday, and committed suicide on Tuesday. I needed to be finally freed from this world.

Let Go and Let God

But during the Saturday evening program, Rhonda

Fleming, the praise and worship leader, did something she had never done before. After leading us in song, she started praying in the Spirit and playing music on the piano. At the same time, she asked all of us to kneel on the plain concrete floor, which was rough and not my idea of fun. Kneeling before a god who had placed me in this world and given me my parents was not something I wanted to do at all. I was mad at God for allowing me to be born. I didn't want to do as the worship leader asked, but I was also afraid that I'd stick out and draw attention to myself if I didn't kneel. So, I knelt like everyone else. Two elderly ladies sitting directly in front of me, however, did not kneel. Because the chairs were lined up in close rows, I was basically breathing down the backs of these ladies' necks and thinking, *I hope this is over fast.* I vaguely recognized the two ladies from a prior retreat, and I knew they were both godly women. In retrospect, I believe the Holy Spirit came upon them during that time of prayer, and because I was so physically close to them, some of the presence of the Holy Spirit must have fallen on me also, somehow, someway.

As I knelt there with my eyes closed, I experienced my very first vision/impartation. All of a sudden, boom! I was shocked to find myself standing alone in the middle of a steel fortress. *What in the world is happening?* I asked myself. As I looked around, I noticed the fortress walls were ten feet high and made of three-inch-thick steel, rusty and black looking. Directly in front of me, the wall had a door with a handle, and there was another wall to my left. Though I only saw the two walls, I knew that it was a square fortress that had a dirt floor. The door of the fortress was solid steel, but in some bizarre way, I could see through it. Stranger still, and to my complete surprise, I saw Jesus Himself walking down a curving dirt pathway directly in front of the main door. I don't know why I knew who it was, but I just did!

Jesus, Angels, Satan, and Demons Are Real

Two large and impressively built angels were at His sides, dressed in white robes just like He was. Jesus' robe went down to His feet, and He had a rope belt around His waist. He had wavy brown hair, a little past shoulder length, a beard and mustache, an olive complexion, and brown eyes. He had a loving, kind, and peaceful countenance about Him. He came up to the fortress door and knocked on it, and I knew somehow, He wanted me to open the door and to follow Him. I was standing directly on the opposite side of the door with my arms crossed, and I said, "No!" Then I told Him, "These Christians I've been with these last two years keep telling me that You love me, but I don't believe it. I want You to prove to me that You love me, and then I'll follow You. Until now, I have survived and existed in a horrible life of neglect, beatings, and sexual abuse, and I don't see why I should follow You. I'm supposed to believe that You put me in this worthless world, and if You did, it doesn't appear to me that You love me either." In the back of my mind, I was thinking all sorts of thoughts about how I was made to feel that surviving my birth was my biggest sin; that I had spent my whole life trying to be perfect in everything to make up for that sin, but to no avail. My parents didn't love me, and it seemed as though no one else did either.

One thing that was running through the back of my mind as all of this was going on was the thought of middle ground, that there might be a place somewhere between heaven and hell if they existed. Heaven maybe existed, but hell, I wasn't so sure of. I knew without a doubt that there was evil in this world, but I thought it was the behavior of mean and angry people. All the therapists I'd been to during the previous ten years had taught me about a middle ground. They wanted me to try and stay there, to avoid extreme swings of my inner pendulum. Also, when I was a child in San Antonio, the Catholic church and school that I attended talked not only about heaven and hell but also about a place they called "Purgatory," which was a middle ground according to them. Previously, I had felt that if God and heaven existed, I surely had been good enough to deserve the last seat in the last row in heaven. It's amazing how fast thoughts can fly through your mind in a moment of crisis.

My thoughts returned to my awareness of Jesus when He knocked again. I spoke up angrily, saying, "No, You prove first that You love me, and I'll think about following You." He knocked a third time, and I repeated with disdain in my voice, "No, I'm not following You," folding my arms in front of me even tighter. After that, He turned around slowly, very peacefully, and started walking away, moving back up the totally barren dirt trail.

In the instant that Jesus turned away from me, I felt the presence of someone else in the fortress with me. To my utter surprise and horror, I saw Satan standing to my left. Again, I don't know how I knew who he was, but I just did. He was dressed in a plain black suit (nothing special, just a black suit) and had long dark hair and sinister eyes. He looked at me with a smirk on his face and said, "You are mine!" My mind instantly flooded with full-blown terror! No! No, this can't be happening to me! I don't deserve to go to hell. How can this be? Fear filled my entire body, and my depression plummeted to sheer despair.

Finally, a light went on inside my head, and my spirit knew that if I didn't choose Christ, consciously and willfully, then I was actually choosing Satan by default. With God, there wasn't any middle ground: I had to make a choice, to either follow Christ or not. How could this be? I looked at Satan, thinking, "No, no, this can't be happening." I then ran to the door to follow Jesus, but it wouldn't open. It was jammed shut. I hit it with my shoulder several times as hard as I could, but it just wouldn't open, and somehow I knew that Satan was keeping it shut. I could feel myself panicking so much that it nearly overwhelmed me. *I'm going to spend eternity in hell*, I thought. I saw a piece of wood like a tree limb lying on the ground, so I picked it up and went at Satan with all the fury, anger, and hatred I held, hitting him right across his abdomen. He bent over a little bit, but then he stood right back up and looked at me with a smirk. I hit him again and again with every ounce of energy and strength I had, but none of it seemed to faze him. "You can't hurt me," he said proudly, easily wiping the dust from the front of his suit. My hands were painful and bleeding from gripping the ruff wood, and my shoulder was sore. I was thinking fearfully; *I'm going to hell because I didn't understand! How can this be happening?* My mind screamed, *This isn't fair!*

Jesus Can Rescue Us

I had never before raised my voice or screamed in my whole life, and I didn't even know if I was capable of screaming. But I did in this vision; I screamed at the top of my voice: *NO! This isn't fair! I didn't know the rules.* I had believed there was a middle ground and that I could sit on a fence post and let these two entities, if they existed, just war it out. I knew only people like the Pope or Mother Theresa were good enough to be in the first row in heaven, but surely, I deserved a seat somewhere there. I surely didn't deserve eternity in hell! In the next moment, I said something that wasn't at all like me, something I'd never said before. The words were just too godly and too Christian sounding. They just formed on my lips, and I looked straight at Satan, and I said with a commanding voice, "Satan, in the name and power of Jesus Christ, be gone from me *now!*"

I Made My Choice

Instantly, Satan was shot up into the sky! It was like some invisible force grabbed him, and the only word I can come up with that fits is that it *catapulted* him up and out of the fort in a mighty arc to the west. Some invisible, tremendous power shot him a hundred miles into the sky and directly into a circular black hole that had suddenly formed above the fort. Even though Satan was far away, being held powerless by some force, I could still see him clearly. Even worse, he could see me, and he looked down at me in extreme anger. I didn't know what to think of these events, and my mind was in pure turmoil. Terror just took over, and I suddenly realized that Satan might retaliate against me. Oh, dear God, what is happening? I asked myself. I need to get out of here; I don't understand what has just happened. As a result, I ran for the door of my fortress before Satan could do something.

I grabbed that same door handle, and to my immense relief, it opened with complete ease. Jesus had stopped partway up the trail and was standing there with the two angels slightly behind Him. He looked at me, and then I noticed a large and extremely bright glow of yellow-white light surrounding Jesus and His angels. I ran up the trail thirty feet and stood just inside this light. This glowing light was ten feet in diameter and had loving warmth to it. I didn't touch Jesus or the angels, but I stood just inside that glowing circle with them.

Jesus turned and looked up at Satan, saying, "Now she has made her decision! She is mine, and you are to leave her alone!" To my amazement, I saw a golden beam of light come out of the tip of Jesus' right first finger. Jesus pointed the beam of light up at Satan, hitting him right in the gut. With a motion of His arm, He hurled Satan backward, deeper and deeper into that horrible black abyss. I can't describe how black the abyss was; it was phenomenally dark and eternally deep. Then two more angels appeared behind me, and Jesus was in front. I was being surrounded, and all of us were in His light. All my fears were totally gone, and I felt wonderfully secure. We then continued walking up the hill, and that is where the vision ended.

In that moment, I honestly thought I was losing my mind! I had never before had anything like this vision happen to me.

I thought my mind had cracked, and I was beginning to worry whether my brain would have enough functioning ability left to find my way back home on Sunday. The praise leader, Rhonda, finished the music, and someone else talked as we sat down in our uncomfortable chairs. But I truly didn't know what to think about my experience. I had read about saints of old having visions from God, but I'd never read about an experience by anyone like me. As a result, I didn't tell anyone about the vision for months. I was also frightened that if I spoke to someone, he or she would determine that I was suicidal and try to have me committed to a hospital again. My next vision/impartation happened about an hour later.

VISION TWO: THE CREVICE

In My Helplessness

Choices Still Have to Be Made

At the retreat, the featured speaker was Pastor Norma Guerrant, whom I knew vaguely from a previous retreat. She resumed talking at the end of my first vision for a short time. We were then given an afternoon break prior to dinner, and Norma waited at the door to greet everyone as they went out. As I approached the old doublewide doors, I tried to leave beside another lady so that I could slip out without being noticed. But as it turned out, Jesus was faster than I was. He had tugged at Norma's heart about me, and she knew from God that there was something wrong. At Jesus' prompting, she reached past the other lady and grabbed my hand. I thought about shaking loose from her grip and excusing myself quickly. But before I could do anything else, she had a hold of my arm and asked me to wait while the hall emptied out. **Coincidence or the Hand of God?** At the time, all I could think was, *Oh dear Lord, no!*

In my struggles to beat my depression, I had been through numerous antidepressant drugs, private and group therapy, hypnosis, prayer groups, read numerous self-help books, went to seminars on positive thinking, spent weeks and weeks in a treatment center, was hospitalized, and finally had electroshock therapy. I didn't want to tell Norma that I was depressed and suicidal because she was an ordained pastor and would be required to report it to the authorities. I really didn't want to talk to anyone at all. But I assumed that if I didn't at least say hello to her, she would know something was amiss and would track me down.

We started talking while we walked in the direction of her cabin. We didn't have to go far, maybe sixty feet and over a tiny bridge that had been built over a now-dry creek bed. Her cabin was one of the oldest on the grounds of the retreat center. We arrived at the dilapidated, crooked, wood cabin with its chipped paint and reached for the door just in time to see a mouse scurry past. After we both caught our breath, she proceeded to open the old door with a slight shove of her hips. We were both glad to be inside, not that it would help much because her cabin had several mouse holes in the walls. As I have mentioned, the cabin was ancient and probably should have been used for firewood. Inside, I sat on her old, dented mattress as she sat on the only chair available in it. She sat down facing me, knee to knee, and we were not talking long before she knew something was terribly wrong with my spirit and mental state. With enough probing, I finally confided in her and told her that I was suicidal.

Then I made her promise on her Bible that she would *not* tell anyone about me. I told her that I'd already been through years of treatment, including a padded suicidal lock-up ward, and that I wasn't doing that again. She gave me her word, and then she begged me to allow her to get two other ladies to pray for me. I immediately thought, *Oh great! More people.* She gave me her word that they would also be silent about my emotional state and intentions. After a bit of time, I said okay, and all she had to do was go to the adjacent cabin to get the other two ladies. All three of them were back before I could chicken out about talking with them. Well, low and behold, she'd enlisted the help of the two elderly ladies I had been kneeling behind during the first vision only an hour earlier. Again I ask, **coincidence or the Hand of God?**

Let Go and Let God

They were also very godly women, not pastors, but they had walked with the Lord for several decades. The three of them started praying for me and continued for two hours. They knew quickly that there was a very strong demonic hold on me. While they prayed, I shared about the intense hatred I had for my mother and father. The ladies wanted me to try and find some forgiveness for them, but my thoughts flooded back to some of the abuses I had endured. My parents beat me numerous times, forced me to lie, used me as currency between the two of them, were untruthful to me, and basically neglected me as a child of twelve years old after their divorce. How could I forgive them? I could not even say the word "forgiveness." I was trying, but honestly and to my surprise, the word would not form on my lips. Every time I tried to say the word "forgiveness," I started gagging heavily, and I was hitting myself on my thighs. I was convinced my mind had cracked after the first vision, so I didn't tell them of it. As the ladies continued praying for me, I had a second vision.

Support Is Out there

In this second vision, I immediately understood that I was in the process of committing suicide. I saw myself inside a very narrow crevice in the earth, and I was hundreds of feet down. I was standing on two little ledges, each about an inch wide, and I knew that fatigue would take over my body soon and that I would fall to my death. Even if I had wanted to get out, I understood that there was no way to escape. I couldn't see any ropes, tools, or handholds, and the walls beside me consisted of dry, crumbling old dirt. I was in there and was about to die very shortly after I or the dirt surrendered to the weight of my life.

Angels Are Real

Again, there must have been some tiny part of me that still wanted to live because without thinking, I lifted a faint whisper to God for help. I was surprised when suddenly, two angels appeared in the crevice in front of me. "What are they doing here?" I asked myself. Honestly, there was only room for the width of one angel's body, but somehow, the walls adjusted. Both angels fitted in the space with me, standing side by side and floating in the air. In the next moment, they told me to step off the tiny ledge and onto their feet. I was startled because I heard them say those words, but I didn't see their lips move.

It was as though ideas went from their mind to my mind. I told them, "No, I'm going to hurt you because I'm heavy." They both smiled and answered with a loving chuckle, "We promise you won't hurt us." After some hesitation, I did what they said. I stepped on the first angel's foot and then onto the second angel's foot. Immediately, we floated upward and came to the top of the crevice.

Jesus Can Rescue Us

I was shocked to see Jesus standing a few feet from the edge. He was dressed, as I had seen Him in my first vision, in a white robe, a belt around His waist, and a kind expression on His face. Somehow as I stepped off the angels' feet, every cell in my body suddenly understood all that Jesus was: His authority, His majesty, His splendor, and His power. I instantly fell face down, flat on the ground in front of Him, and said with tears in my eyes, "My Lord and my God. I have sinned and broken every one of Your commandments, and *I am so sorry!*" Jesus instantly reached down, gently grabbed my hand, and helped me to stand up. We walked twenty feet or so and entered a large white room. As we turned to the right, a huge scroll appeared. This scroll was about ten feet high and just floating in the air. Then it started unrolling in both directions, directly in front of us. After a moment, it stopped, and I could see that it was displaying a section with my sins on it. My heart broke as I saw this list, and I said with all sincerity, "Jesus, I am so sorry!" He looked at me and said, "Your sins are forgiven and forgotten for all eternity," and *instantly*, this section of the scroll that belonged to me simply vanished. Poof! It was gone! The new raw edges came together, and the scroll rolled up from both sides and disappeared.

My mind was swirling, trying to figure out what had just happened; how could all of this be true, how could my sins simply be gone? Jesus took my left hand, and we walked a few steps onto an elevated all-white platform that was at one end of a great hall. When I looked up, I saw what appeared to be a million happy children and teenagers all dressed in white looking at us. Jesus was to the left of me, and He brought me forward and introduced me to this multitude of children. He said, "This is my beloved, of whom I am well pleased." When I heard Him say that, I mentally rebuked Him. *How can you say that about me?* I thought. *I'm nothing. I'm no one!* Jesus instantly turned and rebuked me in return, "You should dare not rebuke the word of God." Jesus' rebuke was spoken with love but with a firm, intense authority. He spoke directly to my mind again, saying, "*I AM!* And *WHAT I SAY IS.*" Then He said, "You will not be the greatest in my kingdom, nor will you be the least." And I spoke back to Him, "I'm sorry; I'm sorry. This is all new. I don't understand what's going on here." He turned again to the multitude and said, "This is my beloved, in whom I'm well pleased."

Within a few seconds, a teenage boy off from the right came walking up four stairs in front of us. He was carrying a small infant girl, about three to five months old. While he approached me, I thought: *No, no, I don't do babies. I never have.* I've always had a weird baby phobia, feeling certain that I'd hurt them somehow. But to my utter surprise, the teenage boy kept coming and didn't say a word. He simply placed the infant girl in my arms, and when I looked down at her, I suddenly realized that she was me! The boy turned and walked back down the stairs, and I was left holding the infant, the infant me. Jesus looked at me and said, "Even though you weren't loved on earth, and even though you weren't cared for by your parents, little Cindy has been cared for and watched over lovingly in heaven."

I was stunned by what Jesus had said, and somehow I knew that it was true. Looking at the infant, I noticed that she was just as happy as she could be. It was difficult for me to wrap my head around the fact that she was me and that she was loved. I just stood there staring at her in awe when I noticed her tiny fingers. I reached down to touch her little hand, and when I did, Jesus reached over to put His right hand on top of mine. Without thinking, I bent over and kissed the back of His hand, and when I straightened back up, I saw the horrible wound in His hand where He had been nailed to the cross. It was over an inch long, with jagged edges, partially open, red, and bruised looking. It looked so terribly painful that my heart just broke. I turned to Jesus and said, "Can I carry the pain of that one wound of yours for a day to free you up for one day? Can I carry it for you?" I just felt so, so badly at the brutality; it was a horrible wound. He had gone through all that in part because of my sins! He turned toward me and lovingly said, "No, my Father in heaven has given me what I need to carry this pain. It's my gift of love to you." Jesus lifted His hand off mine, and as He turned it over, a bright white light came shining up and out of the wound. Then to my further bewilderment, a red rose came out of it, and Jesus took the rose and offered it to me.

Then instantly, the multitude of children started singing a cappella ("Jesus Loves Me"), this I know, for the Bible tells me so. I don't have words to describe how beautiful it sounded! It was angelic, alive, heavenly, and majestic and had a substance about it that I cannot put into words. It was a sound I can't describe here on earth: it was just so incredibly beautiful and alive. When they finished the song, the vision faded.

Prayer Causes Change

When I came out of the vision, the three saintly women were still praying for me. My gagging and hitting myself had stopped. They again asked me to forgive my mother and father, but I could not do it yet. Instead, they then prayed asking the Lord for my heart to have just a willingness to forgive, which I was eventually able to do after an intense struggle. I didn't tell these prayer ladies about either of my visions for months.

I heard one of them quietly say the time and that two hours had passed. My God! They had sacrificed their entire afternoon's free time to pray and do battle for me. I thought, *Wow, Cindy, your mind has cracked! You are a goner.* I was totally wasted, and I had no energy left. I didn't know what to think of all these experiences. Pastor Norma, Mary, and Olivia left me on the lumpy mattress because they could see that I was exhausted. I quickly dozed off and slept peacefully for several hours. When I awoke, I went up the hill to go to dinner, and after that, I went to the meeting hall again.

Rhonda, a professional pianist, was there to lead us in music again, but this time she started the praise time by singing a cappella: ("Jesus Loves Me"), this I know, for the Bible tells me so. My jaw dropped! Of all the thousands of songs she must have known, how could she have picked this one? And why do it a cappella, just like in my vision! I ask you again, **coincidence or the Hand of God?** That just blew me away. I sat in the back, crying my eyes out, but again, I didn't tell a soul what was happening to me.

The retreat ended, and I came home on Sunday evening. Monday, I had planned to get a rifle and then shoot myself with it on Tuesday. Things were ready: I'd written notes and mailed them, and I'd already had my precious animals that I loved more than anyone or anything put down. All my affairs were in order, and I'd even selected the trash bag that I was going to lie in so that I would not make a mess with all the blood. All anyone would have to do afterward was pick me up and toss me in the trash. I didn't want to leave bloody remains with no note and a horrible mess like my older sister had done when she shot herself a few years earlier. But for some reason, I didn't buy the gun. I just spent Monday sitting on my couch thinking about the two visions.

When Tuesday came, I woke up, and for the first time since I was sixteen, the depression was gone. It was like someone had lifted a 1000-pound weight from me. I couldn't explain it. Suddenly everything was basically okay. I wasn't jumping for joy, but I was telling myself, *Wow, things are not too bad!* The air seemed fresher and easier to breathe. There was somehow a quiet peace and serenity within me. It was a strange sensation, not having the weight of that depression on me. And *I didn't commit suicide!* So, I ask you again, **coincidence or the Hand of God?**

After a few months had gone by, I wrote to Norma and told her about the two visions and that my depression was gone. She immediately called me back and was absolutely elated. She was overjoyed! She knew it was of God, by God, and from God, for my depression to be lifted and Satan's demonic hold on me to be broken. She knew that God had plans for me, and she was absolutely thrilled. I proceeded to write the other two ladies, Mary and Olivia, to thank them for their efforts in freeing me and sharing so much love with me. It was months later, after I began reading the Bible, that the Lord started taking me to verse after verse that backed up what He had shown me, taught me, and allowed me to see in those two lifesaving and life-changing visions. I'd like to share some of them with you to help you also understand just how much Jesus loves us, just how much He knows of the events in our lives, and what He is doing about them. I hope that you'll see, in the name of Jesus, there really is power. We do have a choice to make before we leave this mortal body. I pray that you choose to have a relationship with Christ.

The Bible—An Instruction Manual on Living

Although in the first vision, my hardened heart was an old rusty fortress, Jesus still was looking for me. "Behold, I stand at the door and knock. If any anyone hears My voice and opens the door, I will come in to him, and dine with him, and he with Me" (Revelations 3:20, NKJV). This verse surprised me because it is what Jesus did for me. Even today, Jesus is still going from broken heart to broken heart, knocking and asking if He might enter in.

In the first vision while in my fortress, Jesus waited until I was done trying to fight my own fight, and when I realized that I was unable to fix my problem of being trapped there with Satan, He gave my spirit the words, "Satan, in the name and power of Jesus Christ, be gone from me now." "And call upon me in the day of trouble: I will deliver thee, and thou shalt glorify me" (Psalm 50:15, KJV). I needed to realize that I was wrong in my beliefs, for it says in John 8:32 (ESV), "And you will know the truth, and the truth will set you free." I had to learn the truth of having to pick a side, the truth that Jesus and Satan are real, and the truth that Jesus is more powerful than Satan and that Satan is more powerful than we are.

Then Jesus went on to show me that *we do have to pick* a side to follow and that life does *not* end here on earth. "Don't you realize that you become the slave of whatever you choose to obey? You can be a slave to sin, which leads to death, or you can choose to obey God, which leads to righteous living" (Romans 6:16, NLT). Thank you, Father.

And then, just in case my spirit of pride should kick up, and I believed that I had somehow saved myself, He said in Ephesians 2:8–9 (NIV), "For it is by grace you have been saved, through faith—and this is not from yourselves, it is the gift of God—not by works, so that no one can boast." When I first read this scripture, I could feel my entire being agreeing with the meaning because I knew that I had been helpless in my own strength against Satan.

The Lord showed me that my sins had been recorded in

heaven. And then He showed me they were totally gone, absent, vanished out of sight forever. For in Psalm 103:12 (NIV), "As far as the east is from the west, so far has he removed our transgressions from us." Thank you, Lord, for forgiving us and for forgiving me. Then in Psalm 91:11–12 (NIV), "For he will command his angels concerning you to guard you in all your ways; they will lift you up in their hands, so that you will not strike your foot against a stone." Jesus had sent two angels to rescue me from the crevice where I was stuck. For it says in Psalm 30:3 (NIV), "You, LORD, brought me up from the realm of the dead; you spared me from going down to the pit."

In Revelations 3:5 (NASB), it says: "The one who overcomes will be clothed the same way, in white garments; and I will not erase his name from the book of life, and I will confess his name before My Father and before His angels." Wow, what a comforting thought this verse is, my Lord and my God, thank you.

He went so far as to show me the horrible wound in His hand. I'm ashamed to say a part of my spirit must have been in alignment with Thomas, His doubting disciple, because I also needed to see proof. "Then he said to Thomas, 'Put your finger here, and see my hands; and put out your hand, and place it in my side. Do not disbelieve, but believe'" (John 20:27, ESV). "But he was pierced for our transgressions, he was crushed for our iniquities; the punishment that brought us peace was on him, and by his wounds we are healed" (Isaiah 53:5, NIV).

Jesus told me He was "I Am," then He led me to the verse in John 8:58 (ESV), "Jesus said to them, 'Truly, truly, I say to you, before Abraham was, I am.'" Trust me when I say that I was shocked to see these same words in the Bible.

Then, just in case I would take offense on being rebuked by Jesus, He tells us in Hebrews 12:6 (NIV), "My son, do not make light of the Lord's discipline, and do not lose heart when he rebukes you, because the Lord disciplines the one he loves, and he chastens everyone he accepts as his son." As time passed and my connection to the Bible deepened, I slowly began to understand how Christians could celebrate with the words of the Psalms. "I will give thanks to you, LORD, with all my heart; I will tell of all your wonderful deeds" (Psalm 9:1, NIV). A few years later, after more inner healing, I learned to play the guitar and sing in order to become part of a praise and worship team. Many years after that, I took on the responsibility of leading my own praise and worship team. Thank you, Jesus, for the miracle of these changes in my life. So again, I ask you, was all of this **coincidence or the Hand of God?**

While I continue sharing my life and visions with you in the next several stories, I am trying to show you His healing, saving grace, and love for us. He came into my life, the life of a person who was filled with horrible anger, rage, and "un-forgiveness." If He does this for me, I believe He will do it for you. Later, when I contemplated what I had just seen and experienced, I realized that God does not send people to hell; He simply honors their choice. Hell is the ultimate expression of God's highest regard for the dignity of man. He will never force us to choose Him, even when the use of our free will means we would select hell. The choice is up to us! We must choose for ourselves today whom we will serve. This God who spoke still speaks. This God who came still comes. He is here in our world, and He comes to do what we cannot. Thank you, Father, for helping me in my hour of total defeat.

VISION THREE: THE PEPPERCORN SEED

Even a Tiny Piece of Hate

My Choice

It took several months before I shared my first two life-changing and life-saving visions. I had started meeting with the hospital chaplain, where I worked to try and better understand God and his desires for us. The chaplain at my work was an astonishing Christian named Reverend Carmen Warner Robbins. She would get together with me weekly to pray and teach me the truth of the Bible. By this point, I needed to know if things like my visions happen to normal people. I also wanted to know why God would want to save someone like me.

As mentioned earlier, I had told the three ladies who had prayed with me at the retreat about my visions, but now I included a few other godly ladies and several pastors. We would meet, and they prayed with me and then told me to seek out a lady in my church named Gwen Hurst. She was an incredible person who walked closely with God. We became friends, and she spent several hours in prayer with me over the years. She started the arduous task of helping me understand that our God is truly loving and forgiving and that He was not the angry, punishing God that the Catholic Church had taught me to fear as a child.

Let Go and Let God

After a time working with her, Gwen learned the name of a husband-and-wife couple, the Bandals, who were also prayer warriors. She had never met them, but she trusted the person who had told her about them. She gave me their name and phone number and suggested that I call them for prayer. It took a while before I could work up the courage, but eventually, I did set up an appointment at their home. I went on a Friday evening in April 1993 after work and got there at 4:15 p.m. I was forty-five minutes early, so I just sat in my car, mustering up the determination to go in for my appointment.

I know it is going to sound odd again, but I've realized that the Lord somehow uses birds to bring me a sense of peace in times of stress. As soon as I pulled up and parked on the street, a bird flew past and landed on the branch of the tree that I had parked under. The bird was right smack in front of me on a low-hanging branch. While I was praying and wondering what God had in store for me, this bird sat there looking at me. For forty-five minutes, it simply sat there watching me.

Eventually, five o'clock came, and I reached for the door handle. While I was getting out of the car, the bird finally flew away toward the Bandals' house. In a strange way, that bird did help settle my nerves. The Bandals met me at their door and invited me in, and I sat down on a couch in their living room. They sat in two chairs in front of me. They told me that they both had just finished a forty-day fast, only consuming bread and water and spending all the time they could in prayer. *Wow*, I thought. Personally, I had never fasted for one meal. I truly felt I was in the presence of godly and holy people. Nevertheless, I was still hesitant to share my childhood stories of abuse. I felt ashamed and somehow defective and that I didn't deserve their kindness, love, or help. In my mind, I had to be worthless: *Why else would the people in my life have treated me so badly?* My worthlessness and defectiveness seemed to be the only factor that could make sense of their behavior toward me.

Support Is Out There

The Bandals were gentle and loving in their attitude, and they were able to ask the right questions to reveal to them the essence of several different cases of abuse I had suffered. They also knew I had never forgiven any of my abusers. They asked me questions about my childhood, and I answered them the best that I could. I shared with them that I had been an A-B student and had spent my childhood from six to eighteen years old, winning various awards in a desperate attempt to receive love and acceptance from my family. During the earlier years of that time, I occasionally received a little recognition from my parents when I took first place in the two different sports I participated in at the state, regional, and national levels: water ballet and quarter midget racing. If I didn't take first place, I often got disapproval, especially from my father.

I told the Bandals that my parents divorced when I was twelve, and then life seriously changed for the worse. For me, life became a living nightmare when my lying, alcoholic mother started to routinely abuse me physically and emotionally. My mother had two gods, liquor and money, and God help you if you got between her and either of them. To illustrate this point, I saw her point a loaded shotgun at my older brother's face one night because he had stolen just one of her many bottles of booze.

From as far back as I can remember, my mother always made fun of my then pencil-shaped body, which made me painfully shy. When I neared puberty, a total of six men and boys in the neighborhood started sexually abusing me. I made the mistake of telling my mother about one of the men, and the next thing I knew, she took me to the hospital for a rape test. I had no idea what was involved with that test. Worse still, no one at the hospital tried to give me any privacy. Five men stood at the foot of my gurney with my mother and watched the whole exam. I had never felt so violated, ashamed, and humiliated in my life. I literally wished that I could die and wanted to melt into the gurney. After that experience, I knew that there was no way that I was going to tell her about the other men.

I told the Bandals because of my parents' divorce, I was worth $300 in child support to the parent who had me in their care. As a result, the fight began and escalated. At first, I lived with my mother so that my father had to pay the child support fees. My father, who never had a lot of money, was angry that he had to pay for me. He hoped that if I were living with him, my mother would have to pay him the child support. My mother proceeded to lay guilt trips on me night after night, claiming that she couldn't survive without the child support funds. Other times she would say she was saving most of the child support money for a college fund for me. I truly thought she was spending the money on our living expenses. But as time went on, I started asking her why we didn't have food in the house. She told me we just had to make it on her $55 a week she earned working. She would save money in the winter by keeping the thermostat in the 50s, and in the summertime, she wouldn't use the AC. Believe me, it can get very cold and hot in the heart of Texas. Eventually and painfully, I learned that my mother had been hoarding the child support money for herself, and years later, I discovered that the promised college fund was nothing more than another lie.

A year or so after their divorce, my father sent me a plane ticket to visit him and his new family in Virginia. He had already remarried a woman with two daughters, and they had a newborn son. This trip turned out to be another big nightmare for me. Before I left for my visit, my mother spent every evening brainwashing me into hating my father's new wife and her kids. My mother hated my father for divorcing her, and she truly believed that my father's new wife had somehow stolen him away. I went to visit my father with hate in my heart, only to have him begin to brainwash me against my mother. My father wanted me to know how horrible my mother was because she was trying to break up his new marriage. The weeklong visit could not have been any worse.

After I returned home, my mother was obsessed with getting out of me even the smallest details of the knowledge I had about my father's family. She interrogated me about my father's new life almost nightly. When I seemed reluctant to tell her anything about my father's new family, she used a heavy leather belt to try and beat the information out of me. Most of the beatings started during the night after I had fallen asleep and when she was good and drunk. She desperately wanted information that she could use to destroy her ex-husband's marriage.

Prayer Can Cause Changes

I admitted to the Bandals that I lived with a mountain of hatred for my parents and for people in general. After being with them for an hour, they went into deep prayer, asking Jesus to help me find some degree of forgiveness in my heart. Even though my main purpose in coming to see the Bandals was to please Gwen, something deep down inside of me truly wanted to be healed. While the Bandals prayed for me, I asked the Lord to place a large whiteboard in front of my mind. I was willing to let Him tell me or show me, whatever I needed to know, and I had no preconceived ideas as to what would happen. I also had no idea whether God would say anything to me. But in a short time, I unexpectedly started having a vision, but during the entire experience, I could still faintly hear the Bandals praying for me. Occasionally, they would ask me if anything was happening. Surprisingly, I found it incredibly hard to move my mouth and speak to them. It was a very strange sensation, as if I had left my body and no longer had control of it.

In this vision, though, I'm about nine years old, and Jesus was standing a few feet away. I could hear the Bandals praying to the Lord to help me find forgiveness for my mother. My mind started racing; *How could I forgive her, Lord? She was so cruel to me!* I could not even utter the word "forgiveness." Any time I tried to say it, I would feel dry heaves gripping my body. The abuses that I had endured over the years had led to hatred being my best friend. Again, I could hear the Bandals asking the Lord to help me be free from this hatred.

Jesus Can Help Us

In the vision, I stood there for a while, but I finally walked up to Jesus. I was crying, and I reached into the right pocket of my pants and ashamedly pulled out what appeared to be a black peppercorn seed. This seed represented just a tiny bit of the pure hatred I had for my mother. But it felt like so little compared to the mountain of hate that I kept inside me. Full of shame and sorrow and with my head hanging low, I lifted the seed up to Jesus and said, "This is all the forgiveness I can come up with right now."

Jesus smiled and said, "It is okay." *He was truly pleased with my tiniest effort of forgiveness.* He took me by the hand, and we walked a short distance to where a new, sparkling green patch of grass had appeared out of nowhere. *Wow*, I thought, *Where did that come from?* We both knelt down, and He took the first finger of my right hand and poked a hole straight down into the middle of the grass. He took my seed and gently placed it in the hole as if it were truly something special. Then we pushed the grass and dirt back over the hole.

Next, Jesus walked me to the right about five feet to where there was a galvanized water pail. He grabbed my hand, and we both picked it up. We came back to where the seed was planted and poured water on it. Suddenly, our small patch of grass started expanding in a wide circle around the seed. Jesus looked up and ordered the sun to come over and shine on the spot where the seed was planted. To my utter surprise, the sun did as He had ordered, moving in the sky and shining down right on the exact spot. Wow, I was speechless! Within moments, a shoot for a baby tree started to spring up. We just stood there as the grass, and the tree grew larger and larger. I noticed that flowers start to spring up here and there in reds, blues, and yellows.

The seed that we had planted continued to grow rapidly. The trunk had a smooth, scalloped bark and looked as though it was made up of several trees that were all growing in that one spot. Its canopy, now perfectly shaped like a mushroom, covered several acres of land in all directions. The leaves were green and glistening in the sunshine. It was all so fresh, new, and tender. When we walked under the canopy toward the trunk, I noticed some children in the distance playing in this wonderland. They were enjoying themselves under the shade of this enormous tree. They waved at me as if to thank me for this wonderful place, which I thought was odd because I had not created this place. Jesus and I sat down under the canopy and leaned up against the huge trunk, which was now five feet in diameter. The grass was cool to the touch and so new. Sitting there, Jesus placed his right arm around my shoulder, and I snuggled into His side. A beautiful dark brown horse walked up and lowered its head so that I could stroke its nose. It was so soft to the touch. Several dogs were playing in front of us. *Oh, how I love horses and dogs*, I thought. I could hear birds singing, and several flew down so that I could caress their feathers. A red cardinal especially liked me touching it, and another bird landed on the back of the horse. All the animals were tame and playful. I was truly amazed by the love, joy, and beauty that I was experiencing in this paradise. Was this utopia a tiny part of heaven? I don't know. All I know is that I gave Jesus a tiny fragment of the vilest hatred that I held inside me, and He turned it into a small paradise. Incredible! I was absolutely stunned that Jesus could do all of this with one small black seed of pure, extreme hatred. I kept wondering how that kind of change could be possible. How could something as ugly as a seed of hatred be turned into a place so beautiful?

As the vision slowly faded away, I could feel myself sitting back on their couch again. I told them what had happened, and they were delighted and told me that Jesus was too. They explained how forgiveness is often a process, like peeling an onion. It can be a slow process, and each layer of the work that you do can cause many, many tears, but it is well worth it. I was slowly beginning to understand this fact. They said that if I obeyed God in the tiniest things He asks, He would help me experience love. God would accept the ugliness of my sins, even my inability and reluctance to forgive, and still work a miracle. Thank you, Jesus, for this moment of life that bears your awesomeness, your tenderness, and majesty. I truly had difficulty understanding how Jesus could use something so small and ugly as a seed of hatred to create a place of such love and beauty.

The Bible—An Instruction Manual on Living

During my study of the Bible, He led me to the following verse, "Trust in the LORD with all your heart and lean not on your own understanding" (Proverbs 3:5, NIV). And the verse from Matthew 11:28 (NIV), "Come to me, all you who are weary and burdened, and I will give you rest." And what a beautiful place of rest it was!

"Many are the sorrows of the wicked, but steadfast love surrounds the one who trusts in the LORD" (Psalm 32:10, ESV). The Lord surrounded me with a beautiful place of love and joy.

I know that these good things that I had experienced in this vision weren't anything that I'd achieved on my own: they were given in the love of Jesus Christ. I believe that the heartfelt prayers of the Bandals activated God's power in heaven to give me this vision. God blessed the three of us with an understanding of how very much He loves us. For it says in 1 Peter 3:12 (NIV), "For the eyes of the Lord are on the righteous and his ears are attentive to their prayer, but the face of the Lord is against those who do evil."

VISION FOUR: MY STEPMOTHER AND THE DEMON

Jesus Can Conquer Any Demon

My Emotional Storms

It was just a few minutes later when the Bandals asked me more about my parents. I shared that I knew my father wasn't happy about my mother's drinking; in fact, no one was. To explain how bad it could get, I told the Bandals of the night my parents had a huge argument about the divorce that my father wanted. They were both screaming at each other, my mother was drunk, and one of them had a loaded gun. I was terrified. Their fight was so loud and ugly; I ran and hid in a closet crying. I covered my ears in the hope that I would not hear the hateful words and to block out the sound of the gunshot that I was certain I would hear shortly. I just knew somebody was going to die that evening. Thank goodness the gun was not fired. After a while, my father angrily left the house, and I stayed in the closet crying for a long time. Honestly, I was too scared to come out.

The stress of living with my mother, her drinking, and the other abusive things that she did to me eventually made me physically ill. I was completely alone with my alcoholic mother because my married sister lived in another town, and my brother had run away from home. I didn't have any aunts or uncles, and the entire generation that would have been my grandparents had died before I was born. I eventually confided in a lay teacher at my school, that eventually contacted my sister to let her know that I was ill.

Choices Have to Be Made

My sister knew that our mother would never willingly let me go live with my father. At that time, I was thirteen years old and worth $300 a month in child support to my mom. My sister flew to San Antonio on the pretense of visiting our mom, but she had also contacted my father to tell him how sick I was, and together a decision on what to do with me was made. Late on the evening of my sister's visit, she told me I was going to be kidnapped and sent to live with my dad in Virginia. The next thing I knew, she was secretly packing a few pieces of my clothing, then we had to wait for our mother to pass out from her nightly drinking. My sister then took me to an awaiting cab. She was so scared the cab noise would awaken our mother she wouldn't let us close the doors of it until we were a hundred feet down the road. She was so nervous; I could see that her hands were shaking when she lit a cigarette. We got to the airport gate, and I noticed that she kept looking over her shoulder. I assumed that she was looking for the police and my mother. I'd never seen my sister so frightened; I felt horrible for her. She managed to get me on the plane, and then she left. I would not see her again for a couple of years. I couldn't have known, but being sent to live with my father and stepmother was taking me from living in torment and moving me into a different kind of nightmare. I was about to experience a whole new set of abuses.

My stepmother had two young daughters from a previous marriage and a baby boy with my father. Because the bedrooms in their house were full, they made a space for me in a tiny section of their basement. With a metal clothes closet and some sheets, they made me a "room" that measured about nine feet by ten feet. All I had for furniture was a twin bed and a chair, and because it was winter, their unfinished basement had little to no heat. In fact, my water glass froze solid every night. Because it was extremely cold in my "room," I got in the habit of using five blankets on my bed at night and learned how to change clothes under the covers.

It was only a few months before there was friction between this new family and me. From the first visit and for the next five years, I can honestly say that time spent with my stepmother was a nightmare. I quickly learned that my stepmother didn't enjoy having to take care of children. Prior to this marriage, her mother did the cooking, cleaning and usually babysat the grandkids. But now, my dad wouldn't allow this to happen, and my stepmom had to take on all these responsibilities begrudgingly. However, she did seem to enjoy frequently screaming and hitting the kids with her fists, as I watched in horror. I wasn't at all surprised when my stepmother and her kids expressed they didn't want me living with them, and honestly, I didn't want to live there either. Needless to say, I had begun to think that I had been rescued from a red-hot fire and now was living in a sizzling frying pan. I kept telling myself to try and keep some kind of positive attitude. For at least, I had food now and had left my sexual abusers in my mother's neighborhood, and that was a plus.

Demons Are Real

After I shared this part of my life with the Bandals, they started praying. To my surprise, I had another vision of myself at about thirteen years old. I was standing in front of my twin bed in Virginia, and my stepmom was standing in front of the washer and dryer, which were about fifteen feet away in the other half of the basement. She was a big woman, probably 270 pounds, and I weighed maybe 105 pounds. In this vision, she became livid and started screaming at me about something I had done. As she started to walk toward me, suddenly, her face and body morphed into the form of a demon. God help me! I wanted to scream, but I was so scared that I couldn't move. The demon that she had become one with had a human shape and was black, very muscular, and dressed for war. He was wearing thick leather armor and was extremely angry. His mouth was large and round, and inside it, I could see an incredible blackness that was frightening to behold. It was like the black abyss that I had seen in my first vision. It was a blackness not found on earth. The demon's face and my stepmother's face kept interchanging, first hers, then his. The two were one, and both were screaming at me with every bit of their hatred and rage. I was too scared to even breathe. Even though I found it very difficult to speak out loud, I told the Bandals what I was experiencing, and they continued to pray for me.

Jesus Can Rescue Us

Thank goodness in this vision, Jesus suddenly appeared to the right of me in the basement, and He stepped right in between my demon-possessed stepmom and me. He appeared to me as he had in my previous visions: about five feet, ten inches tall with brown hair, an olive complexion, weighing about 180 pounds. He was dressed in a white robe with a golden belt. This time though, Jesus was carrying a six-foot-long, heavy iron rod in His right hand. This spear appeared to be made of rusty old iron with six sides and an arrowhead-shaped point. Jesus stood facing the demon-stepmom combo, but He didn't say a word. He simply took one step toward them, and they reluctantly stepped backward. When they did, two large angels in white robes appeared and walked over to stand next to me. They motioned for me to step back and sit on the edge of my bed, which I did, but I was so frightened. Very shortly though, my spirit/consciousness was floating above this scene, watching the horror take place in front of and below me.

It was strange, of course, that even though I was being exposed to such hatred, I could no longer feel the fear connected with it. I've found that my fears go away when I'm somehow no longer actually in the vision but simply watching the vision from above. Thank you, Jesus.

Jesus took another step toward this demon-possessed stepmom combo, moving them further away from me. She and the demon were still changing faces, and both were blaring hateful words at me. Neither one had any reverence for Jesus at all. They showed total defiance of our Lord's authority. In response, Jesus suddenly lifted His iron rod and skewered both through their chests. Without any apparent effort, He lifted them above his head and flung the pair downward through the floor. For some reason, I could see through the floor to where they were being sent to and was startled to see two huge gates of hell appear. These wooden gates looked like they were made from old railroad ties that were standing vertical and dark brown in color. The stepmom/demon was impaled onto the right gate of hell, still screaming.

I was in shock and speechless while watching these events. Then Jesus turned away from them, and His eyes locked with mine in a loving gaze. I was smiling back at Jesus when I saw movement out of the corner of my eye. The demon-stepmom combo was slowly and painfully trying to move themselves up and off the rod/spear. There was no doubt in my mind that if they escaped, they would return to the basement where I lived. I turned toward Jesus with a quiver in my voice and simply said His name, "Jesus." He looked back down at the skewered pair and made a motion with His hand. Iron bars resembling those of a prison cell suddenly surrounded them, attaching them to the gate of hell permanently. I realized that Jesus had left the rod in the demon's chest as a message, a symbol to the rest of the demonic world that *Jesus is Lord, and He is the most powerful entity of all. He has won victory over the demonic world!* I descended back into my body, where it was sitting on the bed, and the vision ended. I slowly opened my eyes and shared what I'd seen in this vision with the Bandals. Believe it or not, I was still so upset by that demon's anger and what I'd seen that my hands were shaking.

The Bandals asked me to forgive my stepmother, but I wasn't willing. They walked me through a prayer, asking God to help me to be *willing* to forgive her, even this smaller act was not easy for me, but I repeated the prayer with them. God knew that I needed to find the peace of forgiveness with her, and He was more than willing to help me. He had more "peeling of my onion" planned for me in future prayer sessions.

The Bible—A Manual on Living

I had read the Bible once cover to cover, but in the months that followed this vision, I started a deeper search in order to understand the purpose and meaning of what I was seeing. While I did, the scriptures came to life more and more as Jesus spoke to my heart. He led me to scriptures that told me He'd be there in my trials and that I wasn't alone. He said He would fight my battles and win. I was slowly learning to commit every situation to God and to trust Him for the outcome. For the first time in my life, I really began to believe He had been with me throughout those lonely and frightful times.

"The name of the LORD is a strong tower: the righteous runneth into it, and is safe" (Proverbs 18:10, KJV). He showed me that I didn't have to make some big and convoluted prayer to get His attention and help. Just say His name, Jesus!

"Even though I walk through the valley of the shadow of death, I will fear no evil, for you are with me; your rod and your staff, they comfort me" (Psalm 23:4, ESV). Wow, Jesus had a heavy rod in this vision that He used to skewer the demon in my stepmom.

Jesus was kind enough to send two angels to be with me while He took care of the demon. "For he will command his angels concerning you to guard you in all your ways" (Psalm 91:11, NIV). "Say to those with fearful hearts, 'Be strong, do not fear; your God will come, he will come with vengeance; with divine retribution he will come to save you'" (Isaiah 35:4, NIV).

"God is our refuge and strength, an ever-present help in trouble" (Psalm 46:1, NIV). Thank you, Lord, thank you! These scriptures helped show me that when Jesus says He will keep you safe, He means it. I am convinced Satan will have to get through Him in order to get to me. Satan is powerless against the protection of Christ. Jesus has been showing me that He is God and that I can count on Him. He doesn't always keep us from the pains of this fallen world, but He promises to walk with us through them. So, just like broken pieces of colored glass can be used to make a beautiful stained-glass window for a church and aren't useless, He is teaching me that, in His hands, these broken pieces of my life can also be used for something worthwhile. I can honestly say I did not enjoy being broken into pieces by sinful people, but I do hope and pray that some of my pieces can be used to help someone. So again, I ask you, **coincidence or the Hand of God?**

As Jesus was there with me, He is there with you, too. He does know your pain and deepest fears. As the Bible is becoming more real and alive to me, I am seeing how it is filled with life's instructions for joy and happiness. It reveals that we can get through painful valleys of life to reach His mountaintop of peace. Thank you, Jesus! You are an awesome God.

VISION FIVE: MOM, A BELT, AND THE HAND

Beating Meant for Me

I was still in the Bandals' living room, and we gave prayers of thanks to the Lord for what He was revealing to us. They again asked that the Holy Spirit lead and guide everything that was happening that evening and reveal more to me. Then they asked me more questions about my mother and the type of relationship that I had with her. They could tell that just mentioning my mother would cause the anger that I held inside to start burning. They also knew that it was going to take a great deal of time for me to forgive her, for my hate ran deep, and they were right.

My Emotional Storm

As I mentioned, I had a one-week visit with my father and his new family. After this visit and months before my sister kidnapped me, my mother started a nightly routine of trying to beat out of me information about my father's new family. She questioned me again and again about my dad and stepmom and about the visit that I had had with them. She wanted to know anything and everything about this woman. Who was she? Where did she come from? How had she met Dad? What did the woman look like? How old were the kids? Where did they live? What was their address? What did their house look like? She was still falsely blaming this woman for "taking Dad away" from her, but Dad wanted to divorce her for years and had waited until I was older.

I continued to share with the Bandals about my life with my mother and why my anger and hatred at her continued to grow. Before I would walk to school each morning, I'd have to help my mother get dressed and do her hair. After school, I had to pick up the house, do the laundry, yard work, and sometimes help cook if there was any food in the house. Then around 10 p.m. nightly, after my mother was good and drunk, she'd awaken me to watch TV. For some reason, my mother thought that I needed to learn certain things, and she would have me watch television documentaries about Hitler and his death camps for the Jews. Even today, many of those hideous scenes are still seared into my brain.

Making a Choice

Because my mom was fascinated with guns, we had a lot of them around the house. She would have me strip down our twelve-gauge shotgun, clean it, and put it back together at midnight a time or two a week. Other times she'd just grab an old leather belt, come into the bedroom we shared, and start asking me questions. Because I was usually asleep, my wake-up call was the feel of the leather belt hitting me. I can honestly say even fifty years later that I still have body memories of her beatings. Most of these times, I'd lie and say I didn't know the answer to her questions, or I'd give her false information in an attempt to protect my father. This abuse would go on for about five minutes, and then she would leave; however, after ten minutes, she'd come back crying and asking me to forgive her. Then she'd leave and drink more and return later with the belt in hand to start the interrogation all over again. This pattern would repeat a couple of times, several nights a week. It was complete insanity, and needless to say, I got very little sleep.

I always thought it odd that these beatings frightened me more than they physically hurt. Decades later, the Lord would show me why this disassociation from the pain was happening. The body memory of those beatings stayed with me for decades, as my first husband can attest. He would always wake up earlier in the morning than I did. When we were first married and because he was sweet, he'd lean over to kiss me on the forehead to wake me. But I reacted violently at being touched while I was asleep and would butt heads with him, which caused welts on both our foreheads. Ouch! It didn't take long for the wake-up kisses to stop. Bummer! No matter how quickly I tried not to react, I always did. As a result, he changed his behavior and started simply touching my shoulder to awaken me. But even his gentle touch would literally send me jumping out of bed and would scare him. Eventually, he stopped touching me; instead, he would stand at the door of the bedroom and call my name softly and repeatedly until I'd wake. Not the best way to start a new marriage!

Similarly, I've lost count of the little old ladies I scared to death in church after they reached over to give me an unexpected touch. So sorry! Thank the Lord that this reaction has diminished greatly.

The Lord's Faithfulness

Once again, while I was still with the Bandals, I simply asked the Lord for a whiteboard, and I told Him I was willing to look at whatever He wanted me to see. Once more, the Bandals focused their prayers on my trying to find forgiveness for my mother after all the years of abuse. Within a few minutes of prayer, I found myself in a vision again. In this one, I was twelve years old, living in my home of origin in Texas. No one else was living there, only my mother and me. It was late at night, and I was sleeping in my bed when suddenly, I was floating above my bed. This was still a strange sensation and something that I knew I couldn't control. I then saw my mother come into the bedroom, and she was carrying the large leather belt again. As she started swinging the belt, she also started the usual barrage of questions, but there was something different about this night.

In this vision, I saw the right hand of Jesus come into the room and cover my entire body where I was sleeping. Even though my mother swung the belt at me, I could see that she was actually hitting the back of our Savior's wounded hand.

He was taking the sting and pain of every lash. The only thing that I felt was His hand pressing against my body every time she tried to hit me. As I said earlier, I'd always been confused as to why I had emotional memories but no real *physical pain memories* from these beatings. I should have, but I didn't. I had memories of being terrified to be in that room with her; however, I never had physical pain memories of these events.

After seeing this vision, a light bulb went off in my head, and I understood why the physical beatings never hurt like I thought they should have. Wow, now I knew why. Jesus, our Lord, came down and had taken the pain on Himself. Oh, my God, why? These beatings were meant for me; why did You take the brunt of them on Yourself? God, how many times in my life have I cried out, "Where are You? Don't You see what is happening?" Accusing You of never protecting me, never caring. Oh, how wrong I had been! I'm so sorry, Jesus. Many Christian brothers and sisters had told me that Jesus is with us during our trials on earth and that He understands our pains and sorrows. I did not believe it was a literal truth until He had given me this vision. Jesus, thank you for standing with me. What a great God we serve!

This realization brought me to tears, and the vision ended. I still couldn't forgive my mother much, but the Bandals led me in a prayer asking the Lord to soften my heart to be willing to fully forgive her someday. My tears turned into sobs when Mrs. Bandal came over and gave me a motherly hug. Oh, how my soul needed such a hug! It was wonderful but also a little embarrassing because I couldn't stop the flow of my tears.

I gave prayers of thanks to Jesus for showing me again that He has always felt my pain and sorrows. He is always there in the times of our deepest hurts and walks with us through the valley of fear. Jesus had actually shown me how this next verse is so true: "Surely he has borne our griefs and carried our sorrows" (Isaiah 53:4, ESV); it blows my mind how Jesus kept leading me to these verses that I needed to see. Then I read in Psalm 138:7 (NIV), "Though I walk in the midst of trouble, you preserve my life. You stretch out your hand against the anger of my foes; with your right hand you save me." I ask of you, are these two verses and my vision just **coincidence or the Hand of God?**

The Lord has helped heal my heart and mind considerably by showing me this next verse: "I have told you these things, so that in me you may have peace. In this world you will have trouble. But take heart! I have overcome the world" (John 16:33, NIV). I'm slowly learning that having your heart and your mind come into alignment with Jesus is so helpful. Thank you again, Lord.

VISION SIX: THE TAR PIT

Close Brush with Death

At a later visit around April 1994, I was again with the Bandals, and we discussed more of my childhood. I shared with them that, when I was fourteen years old and living with my father, he moved the family from Virginia to Arizona. We left a large city of glitter and lights with a population of several million people and went to a one-horse town of 5,000 people. It had one drive-in, two fast-food restaurants, one high school, one junior high, and two elementary schools. To this day, I can still remember my stepmother's face as she realized where she was going to be living. I truly thought that I could see a demon taking over her expression, as the truth sank in that the glitter and glamor she loved was now gone, and she was stuck in a hot and dry tumbleweed town for who knew how long.

Making My Choice

They bought a house, and for the first and only time in my childhood, I had a bedroom to myself. As time went on, whenever my dad passed me in the hallway for some reason, he thought it was fun to hit my arm with his fist very hard, leaving a large and painful bruise. That is, it was fun for him until I started hitting him back with my fist, giving him a similar size bruise. Eventually, this behavior stopped when he stopped hitting me. We were only in that house for about nine months before we had to move because my stepmother was allergic to everything in that house. As a result, Dad moved the family into a doublewide trailer that had radiant heat instead of forced air heat, hoping to reduce her allergy problem.

They bought a mobile home, but it didn't have a bedroom for me. So, my father built a concrete block room/garage onto the side of the doublewide trailer. This brick room didn't have heat, air conditioning, insulation, finishing touches, or a bathroom. The room did have the washer and dryer in it, but my stepmother, in her hatefulness, refused to let me use either of them. In addition, she kept me locked out of the house now. Once again, I was given a single bed, a metal clothes closet, a curtain made from cloth and cardboard, and I recall that I had a couple of bricks and a board for a desk.

Then, my stepmother had me lie about my age so that I could start working when I was fifteen years old. My job was thirty hours a week, earning $1.15 an hour at one of the only two fast-food hamburger joints in town. It became clear to me that my stepmother didn't want me living with them, so she set about making more of my life a living nightmare. It was her way to get back at my dad for moving her and her kids to this pitiful little tumbleweed town.

With my earnings of $30 a month, my stepmother told me to buy myself a car, feed myself, and pay for any medical bills, schooling, gasoline, insurance, clothes, and laundry. She was not going to spend a penny on me, and she made sure that I was not given a key to the house so that I didn't have access to the kitchen or bathroom. I was allowed, though, to use the yard for my bathroom needs with the family dog. Use your imagination: it was never a glamorous situation. After I came home from work, which was near midnight, I got in the habit of using a tiny sink in the garage for my bathroom needs, bathing, and handwashing my clothes. I'm certain that, if she had been awake, she would have stopped me from using even the sink in the garage. I worked from 5 p.m. to 11 p.m., five days a week, and if I wanted to date, we had to meet after I got off work. On my days off, she would have her kids get out their drum set or play loud music to keep me from sleeping or studying. She would not allow me to stay on the property for any reason; this meant that I had to drive twenty minutes into town and stay in my car. Because my car was small and didn't have air conditioning, I was never comfortable and rarely got any of my much-needed sleep.

Just to be clear, I was never a discipline problem. I didn't drink, smoke, use drugs, or have sex. I stayed on the Dean's honor roll and was still winning trophies. I was captain of the volleyball team, president of the school's athletic association, and was picked as the MVP two years in a row. I was a member of a Bible study group and was chosen as the most outstanding student in November of my senior year. I was also awarded one of only two fully paid, four-year scholarships to the Air Force Academy, but because of circumstances, I turned it down. I even tried, through mail-order courses, to graduate a year early, but I nearly died of pure exhaustion from the attempt.

I finished sharing with the Bandals all the hatred I had for my stepmom. And then also my dad, in part because he never protected me from my stepmom. They then led me in a prayer for God to help me, hand over this deep hatred and shame I lived with. They asked for the Lord's mighty hand to touch me with His grace and to give me strength to face my past. While their prayers continued, I soon had another vision. In it, I was seventeen years old, still in Arizona, and I was trapped in a hideous ten-foot diameter pit in the dirt right outside the garage. The pit was filled with a substance that looked like thick black tar, representing pure evil. I was sinking in it and was barely able to hold my head above the revolting substance.

Because my mother was a swimming coach, I had learned to swim by the age of four. In this vision, though, I found it odd that I could not swim out of the vile pit. Having been a champion swimmer, I couldn't believe I was about to go under and drown. Just when all hope was lost, an angel suddenly appeared. He was robed in white, had wings, a fair complexion, and light brown hair that was shoulder length. He looked young, somewhere between twenty to twenty-four years of age, and had the most beautiful blue eyes. He came over to me and knelt next to the pit. Then he placed his right hand under my head to hold it up and positioned himself so that his body and wings covered me. I was awestruck by his wondrous beauty and the look of love in his eyes. Then all at once, there was a multitude of demons coming out of my dad's and stepmoms' trailer and garage with clubs and other bat-like objects in their hands. They were headed for me and wanted to hit me and force me under, to kill me. But the angel who was literally face-to-face with me started taking the blows on his own back that were intended for me.

As I've mentioned before, sometimes I felt like I was participating in the vision, and sometimes I was watching it from a safe distance above the action. At that moment, I was in this vision, in that vile pit, and I was staring into the angel's handsome face. He had such a look of caring about him. His eyes were so vibrant blue that I kept looking at him and saying, "Why are you taking this beating for me? I don't understand. Where did you come from? Why do you care so much?" I'm amazed how many thoughts can run through your mind in a moment. A few seconds later, I floated above this scene, watching while the demons kept coming. They were pouring all their anger into beating this angel to get at me. The blows were so intense that a red fluid, looking like blood, started appearing on the angel's back and wings. By some means, the demons' blows were injuring him.

Jesus Is Faithful

At that moment, the Bandals then asked me a question, and again I found that it was phenomenally difficult to speak to them. Somehow, I managed to slowly tell them what was happening. They refocused their prayers, and then Jesus suddenly appeared in this vision. Just His presence was enough to cause these lesser-ranking demons, as I called them, to flee like they were on fire. Boom! They disappeared in every direction, never to be seen again.

Jesus and two angels walked over to the disgusting pit and helped the angel and me up and out of the tar pit. As soon as I was out of the hideous pit, the tarry substance which was made from vile hate just fell off of me, and I was instantly clothed in a white dress. Then a concrete bench, like the kind you might see in a small city park, appeared about ten feet away. Jesus led us over to it and sat down with the first angel on His right side and me on His left. Jesus put His arms around both of us, and I could immediately feel His love radiating in me. He was very happy and thrilled with His angel and what he had done to protect me from the evil spirits. There was such a sense of peace and love being in Jesus' presence. We sat there for some time, and then the vision faded.

Prayers Can Cause Change

While I gathered my thoughts, I shared with the Bandals what had happened, and they were both thrilled. They shared with me that the empire of angels is as vast as Gods' creation all around us. If you believe in the Bible, you will believe in their ministry to and for us. We all gave thanks to God for showing me that, even in my darkest hour, He was aware of my predicament and had sent me help and comfort. As a result of the Bandals' continued prayer support and the Lord's grace, I was finally able to forgive my stepmom. Having seen her being possessed by a demon in the earlier vision helped make the process of forgiving her much easier.

I found great comfort when I was led to read the following verses: "For he will command his angels concerning you to guard you in all your ways" (Psalm 91:11, NIV). The angel above me completely protected and shielded me from the demons. Absolutely none of them were able to strike me with their weapons. I ask you, how can I not believe in what His word says?

As I continued my Bible reading, the Lord continued to show me verses that confirmed how much He loved me, for it says in Psalm 91,

> I will say of the LORD, 'He is my refuge and my fortress, my God, in whom I trust.' Surely he will save you from the fowler's snare and from the deadly pestilence. He will cover you with his feathers, and under his wings you will find refuge; his faithfulness will be your shield and rampart.
>
> Psalm 91:2–4 (NIV)

Then, in Psalm 40:2 (ESV), I was shocked to read, "He drew me up from the pit of destruction, out of the miry bog, and set my feet upon a rock, making my steps secure." Wow, incredible, that is just what happened to me! So again, I ask you, **coincidence or the Hand of God?**

The Bible kept ministering to me. For it says in Psalm 69:14 (KJV), "Deliver me out of the mire, and let me not sink: let me be delivered from them that hate me, and out of the deep waters." Jesus did keep me from sinking in the mire and prevented the flood of demons from attacking me directly. Then I read in Psalm 34:18 (NIV), "The LORD is close to the brokenhearted and saves those who are crushed in spirit." I could truly relate to this verse, having felt so humiliated and defeated by my family throughout much of my life.

So, I pray for you to not let the burdens and hardships of this life discourage you. Please keep your eyes firmly fixed on what God has promised us. Those who accept Jesus as their Lord and Savior know He has heaven awaiting us. This is a place beyond man's imagination! I now have a much deeper understanding of what these promises mean for all of us. Jesus has sent His angels to care for me, His Holy Spirit to dwell in me, His church to encourage me, and His word to guide me. Thank you, Lord.

VISION SEVEN: BEATEN BY MY DAD

Strange Belt Marks

Around September 1994, I was strongly aware that I still needed to complete the work of forgiving my dad and my mother. By now, I had been going to church regularly and knew a couple more prayer warriors. I invited two Pastors, Don Crary and Jim Hill, plus two laywomen whom I had met, to come over to my house and help me with this process of forgiveness. They were able, through prayer, to help me peel more of my emotional onion of hate and un-forgiveness away. Because we were all new to each other, they asked me questions about my childhood and my home life, trying to determine which parent they should pray about first. I shared with them that my hatred for my father was so deep that I had wanted to kill both him and my mom some years earlier.

I never really felt that my father wanted kids or liked them very much. He almost always called them "rug rats." Because of a lack of funds, he was never able to achieve his dream of becoming a racecar driver. Through a raffle at his work, however, he won two small racecars called "quarter midgets," which were similar to a go-cart. He eventually involved all three of us kids in racing. Because he was a very good mechanic, he had the skill set to have each one of us winning races, giving him bragging rights. My older siblings, sister and brother, started out years before me, but at age five, I started driving. I won my first Texas state championship at the age of seven. Eventually, my sister and brother were too old to race this type of car, and I was the only child who was racing.

Even though all of us kids won race after race, he wanted more, and injury or sickness was never an excuse not to race. In fact, I had flipped my car during a practice session the day before a state championship. Both of my arms were badly skinned up, but he washed them off, wrapped them up with gauze, and had me get back in the car. I won the state championship the next day, which gave him his bragging rights again. I had taken first place at numerous local races, state and regional championships. I also won the right to enter three national races by the time I was twelve, and I placed in the top three spots in two of these nationals. During this same period, being that my mother was the coach of the swim team, I was also swimming and winning numerous medals at the local, state, and regional level in water ballet (synchronized swimming) competitions. Once, I was made to swim with 102 fever and a horrible ear infection during a swimming show. These shows were put on about two to three times per year.

No Good Choice

A year or so after being sent to my dad's, I came home

to visit my mother. As my mother's abuse restarted again, I eventually confided in my girlfriend's mom and dad, who were my God parents, about my living condition at home. They were willing to open their home to me, but they needed my father to send the child support money to them. Neither my mother nor my father would agree to this arrangement. My dad was so angry at this idea that he gave me a frightful and humiliating tongue lashing over the phone; I was then too afraid to go back to him. So, I chose to stay with my mother, that is, until I was kidnapped a second time.

My older brother came into town this time, kidnapped me right out of my 8th-grade class at the Catholic school, and hid me in a closet in his in-laws' home. My mother was furious and had called the police, but they ended up searching the wrong house. In the middle of the night, my brother put me in the back of his station wagon, covered me with a blanket, and drove me back to Arizona to live with my dad and stepmom again. After I arrived there, my stepmom's abuses continued to grow, as did my hatred for her and my father. In the end, I learned that the demonic had its hold on my parents and me. I shared with my prayer warriors about my father's membership in an organization in Texas that they felt was actually associated with the occult. I also told them that a close family friend of my mother's had shared a suspicion that my grandmother or great-grandmother had practiced witchcraft. In addition, when I was much younger, I had unknowingly dabbled in the occult by going to fortune tellers, getting my palms read, looking at tarot cards, viewing pornographic DVDs, and playing with an Ouija Board.

After they heard these details, the prayer team led me in numerous prayers to renounce the satanic and all occult practices for my family and myself. They led me in prayers of reaffirmation of my baptismal vows, and then we shared Holy Communion before we preceded any further. They knew I had to break my connections to the occult before I would truly be able to forgive my father. I told this prayer team that, in an earlier prayer session, the Lord gave me a short vision concerning my father. I had seen a line of people that represented my family going back ten generations. They all had demonic spirits on them or in them. My father was there with five demonic spirits attached to him. One had him by the throat, one was on each arm, and one was on each leg. The team prayed for the Lord to set him and the others free. Suddenly, the Lord appeared with a mighty sword and went about cutting each one of the demonic spirits off these ten generations of my ancestors and my father. This prior vision had helped me understand why my dad was the way he was and why he had not been there for any of us kids.

Now being back with my dad and stepmom in Arizona, I was fifteen years old and back in school as the abuses restarted. In time I again confided in a teacher about the turmoil that I was forced to live in, and he and his family graciously wanted to legally adopt me. I was more than happy about the prospect of living with his family, but he left it up to me to tell my father. After a few days, I finally worked up the nerve to tell my dad about this teacher; with hearing this, my dad went into a full-blown rage. He wasn't angry that I would be leaving again: he was fearful and furious that I had revealed some ugly family secrets. He was angry that someone knew about the abuses that I suffered and his alcoholism. I'm sure he was frightened that he would have to come up with child support again or court fees for the adoption to go through.

The next thing I knew, he was coming back into my bedroom with a wide leather belt. My stepmom was right outside the door with her kids so that they all could have a front-row seat to the beating that I was about to receive. I stood up as he entered my room hollering, and he immediately started swinging the belt, stroke after stroke, for what seemed like an eternity. I was deeply humiliated because I could hear his wife and the kids giggling. What made it even worse was that he forced me to apologize to my stepmom for embarrassing the family by confiding in a teacher. I was ordered to go to school the next day and tell the teacher that there wouldn't be an adoption. I also had to say that everything I had shared with him had been a lie and that he needed to forget everything I had told him. Because my dad had beaten and shamed me so much, I did exactly what he wanted me to do the next day. I don't know which hurt worse: the beating, having to apologize to my evil stepmom, or going to the teacher who cared about me and lying to him. I had to tell him that I had made up the whole story, that everything was just peachy, and that we had a wonderful family. Well, thank goodness; the teacher knew something had happened to make me change my story. He knew that I was lying to him now, but he unwillingly had to let everything drop. He stayed as a secret close friend and confidant throughout the years to follow.

The next several days at school, I had to wear long-sleeved clothes to hide the bruises and red belt marks. I found PE class especially difficult because it was mandatory for us to take a group shower after class. But there was no way that I was going to undress and let anyone see the belt marks. Even though the PE teacher was threatening to give me a bad mark for that day, I was too ashamed about all of it. Instead, I waited until everyone was done in the shower, ran in there quickly, got dressed, and headed off late to my next class. But while I was getting dressed, I noticed something odd in the mirror. I could only find belt marks on my sides and back, not on the front of my body. I kept replaying the beating in my mind's eye, and I knew that nothing had come between my dad and me during that time. Why were there no marks on the front of my body? My dad had used a long belt that wrapped around me every time that he swung it. I struggled to make sense of that strange circumstance, and that question stayed in the back of my mind until decades later when the Lord would answer it for me.

Support Is Out There

While I was sharing this memory with the prayer team, they started to pray, and I experienced another vision. In this new vision, it was the scene of the above incident with changes, though. This vision started right after I had told my father that a teacher wanted to adopt me. I was in my bedroom, as mentioned sitting on the edge of my bed. My father was about to come back to my room when suddenly, I saw Jesus instead walk into my room. Jesus sat down on the bed right next to me and held my hand. Within moments, my very mad father appeared with a belt. When he did, Jesus and I stood up, and Jesus gently placed my face into his chest. He was chest-to-chest with me, and He had His back toward my father. He was holding me gently and hiding my face so that I could not see what was coming. In the next second, I was then floating above the scene, watching it again. Then my father wildly started swinging his belt, but it was hitting Jesus on his back first, and then the tail end would whip around to hit my body. While I was floating above my body, I could see Jesus flinch with each lash of the belt. He felt it: He felt the sting and the pain of the hit. It hurt, and I could tell that He was hurting with me. Jesus stayed with me until the beating was over and my father had left the room.

That's where this vision ended. I once again found myself crying huge tears, but I also felt a sense of comfort because I knew that Jesus really did care for me. He had been there, and He knew what had happened. Knowing that Jesus had been with me as a child, and on into my teens through all these terrors, as I said, made me swell up with tears and cry my eyes out. I shared this vision with the prayer team and my new understanding of the odd belt marks that I had received. Being I had always wondered how it was that I didn't have any marks on the front of my body, now I knew why. Thank you, Jesus, for being with me; You are so merciful. They were all delighted, and we offered gratitude to Jesus for being a God who cares and understands about our sufferings. So I ask you, why didn't I have any belt marks on the front of my body? Was it **coincidence or the Hand of God?**

As the prayer team continued to explore my past, I shared with them that the anger and hatred at my dad and stepmom continued to grow while living with them. As a senior in school, I still had a job, a car, and had found a place to live on my own after graduation and a college to go to. As stated, my dad had placed a dollar value on my head, plus he didn't see enough value in me to protect me from my stepmother. This was so evident as he stepped aside and allowed my stepmother to force me out of the state of Arizona without warning, twelve hours after I graduated high school. I couldn't see any of my friends or say goodbye, and I had to drive to California with two hours of sleep and stay with my older sister. Because I held a mountain of hate in my heart, I knew that forgiving this man was not going to be easy. This prayer session was just the start of several gatherings where we asked the Lord to give me the willingness to forgive him. I'm ashamed to say that I needed to go through a *number of prayer sessions* before I was able to fully forgive my father. Eventually, however, as Jesus healed my heart, I was able to release my hate at him. So much so that I eventually had a heart of compassion for him. In fact, years later, after a third wife of his had died, he needed help to move across the country. My new husband, Fred, and I flew to Georgia, to where he was living. We and others helped pack up my dad and move him back to Arizona. Fred and I then went to Arizona to get his new home ready to move into. We ended up spending five days and a good deal of money getting a shockingly trashed-out doublewide trailer he had purchased repaired and ready for him to move into.

Some years after his move back to Arizona, the Lord prompted me to take my dad on a six-hour drive to see the Grand Canyon. This would provide me the opportunity to witness to him and lead him to the Lord, which I did. He died shortly thereafter when he took a fall and broke his hip. The Lord tested me once again as I was the only speaker at his funeral, and I had to pay for it. Months later, for a time, I even helped his now fourth wife with certain living expenses.

Even as I am writing these words, I'm still amazed at how God gave me the willingness and the strength to forgive this man and give him considerable financial support. With His love and grace, I was transformed from someone who wanted to give my father a bullet between the eyes to someone with a heart that cared enough to help him physically, financially, and spiritually. Again I ask, **coincidence or the Hand of God?**

The Bible—A Manual on Living

For it says in Hebrews,

> For He [God] Himself has said, 'I will not in any way fail you *nor* give you up *nor* leave you without support. [I will] not, [I will] not, [I will] not in any degree leave you helpless *nor* forsaken *nor* let [you] down, (relax My hold on you)! [Assuredly not!]'
>
> Hebrews 13:5 (AMPC)

Before my dad re-entered the bedroom in my vision, Jesus was there with me, and He stood between the belt and me, taking the beating before I did. Then it says in Deuteronomy 31:6 (NLT), "So be strong and courageous! Do not be afraid and do not panic before them. For the LORD your God will personally go ahead of you. He will neither fail you nor abandon you."

"God is our refuge and strength, an ever-present help in trouble" (Psalm 46:1, NIV). Jesus sat with me on the bed, holding my hand, even though He knew that my father would return with a belt. I ask you, would even your closest friend do that for you?

"Surely, LORD, you bless the righteous; you surround them with your favor as with a shield" (Psalm 5:12, NIV). When Jesus says He will keep you safe, He means it. Satan will have to go through Him to get to you. Jesus is able to protect you. Satan is powerless against the protection of Christ!

"Behold, God, my salvation! I will trust and not be afraid, For the LORD GOD is my strength and song; Yes, He has become my salvation" (Isaiah 12:2, AMP). Knowing that the Lord was with me has lifted so much heartache off my chest. For it says in Psalm 34:18 (NIV), "The LORD is close to the brokenhearted and saves those who are crushed in spirit." Thank you, Jesus.

VISION EIGHT: THE DINGY AND THE WIRE

My Secret Escape Route

In August 1995, I was at my house with three prayer warriors and two pastors. We were at my kitchen table working on my numerous resentments toward people. I was still battling with my anger, especially towards those whom I knew that I hadn't forgiven from my early adulthood and my first marriage.

After some intense prayer, another vision began, and I saw myself in the middle of the ocean in a worn-out, beaten down, old dinghy with peeling paint. The boat had a small mast, and the sail was a wind-worn piece of cloth. Because there wasn't a cabin on the boat, everything was open to the sun and wind. I saw myself lying in the bottom of the dinghy near death; my body was blistered and sunburned. I was totally exhausted and out of food and water.

My mind told me that this dinghy represented the real world where I was stuck in my resentment. I had been striving to find happiness and peace in my life, but both continued to slip through my fingers. As a result, my hatred had grown all around me, like the waters around the dinghy. This big, ugly, harsh ocean had me in its grasp, and it wasn't going to let me go. My struggle with existence had taken its toll on me, and I just wanted to lie back and wait for death. I was done trying, done with people, and done with this world.

Making a Choice

While I was drifting in and out of consciousness, I noticed a huge white cruise ship with a number of people on board headed in my direction. The ship changed its course in order to come alongside my dinghy, and I could hear the passengers calling to me. They saw my condition and hollered for me to grab the rope ladder that they dropped over the side of the ship. Because I still had a mistrust of people, I hesitated for a while as the ship continued to parallel the course of my dinghy. Then somehow, I knew that the cruise ship was filled with Christians; with some hesitancy and a secret plan, I eventually gave in to their eager invitations.

Because I still wasn't completely certain that I could handle their Christian way of life, I had kept a tiny spool of fine titanium wire with me. I had hooked one end of the wire to the front edge of my dinghy, and when the passengers were not looking, I secretly walked to the back of the cruise ship to carry out my plan. I attached the other end of the wire to the ship, letting out just enough wire so that the dinghy could drift far enough away that no one would see it. This little boat was going to be my planned secret escape route if things did not work out on the cruise ship.

Because my Christian walk was so new, I felt that I hadn't

been willing to give more than 95 percent of my life to the Lord. The dinghy represented the other 5 percent that I was not yet willing to release. It was my ace in the hole, in case Christianity was a bust. I would get back in my dinghy and let fate run its course, die, and be done with life. My two decades of war, battling depression and suicidal thoughts, had left a huge hole in my soul. Even though my generous prayer warriors and I had made large strides to fill in some of this hole, I felt that a sizeable piece was still missing. I had accepted Jesus as my Lord and Savior at a high school revival when I was sixteen. Though shortly thereafter, Satan started whispering and then screaming in my ear for me to kill myself. I could hear Satan whispering in my ear, "If God really loved you, life would be easier."

Support Is Out There

Having been raised in the Catholic Church, I had been taught that God was a vengeful, angry entity who was just waiting for us to be engaged in mortal sin to send us to hell with no questions asked. This deeply ingrained fear caused me to lose more than a few nights of sleep, waiting for the confessional to open in the morning at school. But when I went to college to get my RN degree, I met a classmate who was a very gracious and strong Christian named Lynn Bailey. We became close friends, and she spent nearly five years helping me undo that Catholic teaching. Over the years, she would call me long distance from Georgia every week to pray with me. She sent me a Bible and scriptures, re-educating me to the truth of God's love for us.

Plus, I had the added blessing of Reverend Carmen Warner Robbins meeting with me once a week to pray for me as well. If I hadn't had both of their steadfast friendship, now lasting over forty years, and their willingness to share God's love with me through prayer, I would not be here today.

The Lord Is Patient

The passengers on the cruise ship reminded me of Lynn and Carmen, and I was being loved and treated very nicely by these new Christians. I was learning the truth about how God really did care for me and that the Bible was filled with good news for the Lord's children. When I read the Bible now, I see a forgiving, loving God who sent His Son to pay for my sins, mortal and otherwise. Life was getting better and brighter. I was finally able to throw away my mental tapes, and I began to believe the truth of the Bible. The cruise ship was a little piece of paradise, and it had most of what I needed. I could feel the desire for suicide and death losing their hold on me. The vision ended when I walked inside the cruise ship to hear more of the message that the Lord had for everyone, including me. Thank you, Lord, for giving me a chance.

Let Go and Let God

These prayer warriors and I met again about three months later. My heart told me that it was time to fully (100 percent) give up my old ways and follow the Lord's way. With the Lord's help and their prayers, I was finally able to go to the back of the cruise ship, pick up that titanium wire, and cut my dinghy loose. This tiny path to death I secretly held onto I would never again reclaim. My heart, soul, and mind were 100 percent the Lord's. With tears running down my face, I apologized to the Lord for not trusting in Him fully. My hands were shaking, and it felt like I had taken the biggest leap of faith in my life. And indeed, I had, for me to totally trust God was an enormous leap of faith. My life was His to use as He saw fit. My faith had changed from the belief that God would do what I wanted to knowing that God would always do what was right for me. I had finally learned that faith with no effort is not faith at all. God has never rejected and will never reject a genuine gesture of faith. I still didn't fully understand that all the pains in my life had actually been caused by sinful choices, mine or someone else's. But now I was seeing that Jesus had been with me and beside me in my darkest hours, not just looking down from heaven and watching them happen to me.

The Lord Is Faithful

I tearfully gave God and my prayer warriors my word that I would never consider suicide again. I must admit it: this was a good feeling but also a strange one. Wow! I had never thought about growing old or planning for the future. This commitment was frightening but, at the same time, quite exciting. Now I had a life, and with God's help, I needed to make some plans for it. I had to trust God because I didn't know what to do about my future. Some people say faith is a desperate dive out of a sinking boat of human effort and a prayer that God will be there to pull us out of the water. I can testify He was there to give me a new life, a new future, and a renewed faith in Him. That's where the second part of this vision ended. The prayer warriors and I were in tears, giving thanks and praise to the Lord.

We were rejoicing that I had made my mind up to never let Satan take hold of me again. With God's help, I was never going to allow Satan to convince me that my life was worthless because now I knew better. I was beginning to understand how much God truly loved me and that He has been and always will be there for me. God, my Father, who is filled with compassion, is very fond of all His children and only wants to share His love with us. Also, I realized that there is an unseen reality around us; some of it is good and some bad. I was learning that I always needed to stay in a relationship with Jesus and to continue a fellowship with my new Christian family. Thank you, thank you, Jesus, for saving me! Romans 15:13 (NIV) took on a new meaning for me; for it says: "May the God of hope fill you with all joy and peace as you trust in him, so that you may overflow with hope by the power of the Holy Spirit." As I put my whole heart in Jesus' strong but tender hands, it was the first time in my life I was beginning to deeply feel His peace, love, and hope for a future.

After some years had passed, I asked Reverend Carmen and my friend Lynn to re-baptize me. This they did with many of my prayer warriors there in attendance. Lynn was so gracious to fly from Georgia to San Diego for the event. She and Carmen are one of a kind, for they walk hand in hand with the Lord Jesus. Thank you Lord, and love to both of them. Jeremiah talks about finding the Lord if we seek Him with our whole hearts. I couldn't do that until I took the part of my willfulness that was still wired to that dinghy, cut it loose, and placed 100 percent of my heart in His hands. Then I could fully believe His word and that He did have a plan for me.

> 'For I know the plans I have for you,' declares the LORD, 'plans to prosper you and not to harm you, plans to give you hope and a future. Then you will call on me and come and pray to me, and I will listen to you. You will seek me and find me when you seek me with all your heart.'
>
> Jeremiah 29:11–13 (NIV)

The Bible—A Manual for Living

"I will be glad and rejoice in your love, for you saw my affliction and knew the anguish of my soul. You have not given me into the hands of the enemy but have set my feet in a spacious place" (Psalm 31:7–8, NIV). When I gave over 100 percent of my will, my heart, and my thoughts, I could finally feel gladness and joy freely moving through me. I knew I was now on a ship that would never experience a disaster or require anything ever again.

> Teach those who are rich in this world not to be proud and not to trust in their money, which is so unreliable. Their trust should be in God, who richly gives us all we need for our enjoyment. Tell them to use their money to do good. They should be rich in

good works and generous to those in need, always being ready to share with others.

1 Timothy 6:17–18 (NLT)

Some people have rejected this, and their faith has been shipwrecked.

"Trust in the LORD with all your heart and lean not on your own understanding; in all your ways submit to him, and he will make your paths straight" (Proverbs 3:5–6, NIV).

"If anyone would come after me, let him deny himself and take up his cross and follow me" (Mark 8:34, ESV).

"All of God's revelations are sealed until they are opened to us by obedience. You will never get them open by philosophy or thinking. Obey God in the things He shows you and instantly the next things are opened up. With the tiniest fragments of obedience, the heavens open and the profoundest truths of God are yours straight away."[1]

> Into your hands I commit my spirit; deliver me, LORD, my faithful God. I will be glad and rejoice in your love, for you saw my affliction and knew the anguish of my soul. You have not given me into the hands of the enemy but have set my feet in a spacious place.

Psalm 31:5,7–8 (NIV)

Thank you, Father.

From *My Utmost*, page 284.

VISION NINE: THE HOUSE AND THE ROCKS

The Lord Has Paid for Our Sins

In January 1996, I was visiting the Bandals again and sitting on their couch. I had become comfortable there; it was like a mini home away from home. I was growing very fond of them both because of their tremendous willingness and love in helping me find peace. They asked a few more questions about my past and again started praying for Jesus to help me find the strength to continue my process of forgiveness. We had made progress with my ability to forgive my mom and dad, but I still had anger at mankind in general.

I was in my 40s before I could let any man with gray hair touch me because of the sexual abuses that I suffered as a child between the ages of ten to twelve years old. Plus, during the nearly ten years that I sought professional help, I'd also been taken advantage of by therapists who were not on the up-and-up. Instead of helping me with my depression, these so-called professionals only made me angrier with humankind. One therapist, who was supposedly a Christian, manipulated me into loaning him money, and I ended up taking out a second mortgage on my house to give him $27 thousand. After a year, I finally realized that this request had been horribly wrong, and I reported him. He ended up losing his license, his job and spent time in jail. This series of events made me feel horribly guilty, and I needed therapy to recover from those emotions, but I was eventually repaid the debt! I had also been in the care of two other questionable Christian therapists, who recommended one thing but did something quite different. One of them claimed to be a good Christian but was in a homosexual relationship with a patient in my group. A third therapist, whom I saw, charged me questionable fees during my therapy. Because of these unprofessional behaviors, I lost faith in them and had to find a different therapist again. I was furious at these therapists who had not lived up to their code of ethics. Too many people had placed their dishonoring sinful acts on me to carry. These types of incidents prevented me from trusting people in general. I discussed these and similar issues with the Bandals so that we could deal with their contributions to my intense anger and shame.

Very quickly after the Bandals began praying, I was given another vision. In it, I was approximately twenty-five years old and had been living in an old, wooden farmhouse in the country. It was painted white, with a porch and stairs that led down to a brick walkway. A small picket fence surrounding the property and a dirt road passed by in front of my place and then turned south. The house was nothing big or fancy, and it was a little run down. In the front yard, I had my vegetable and flower garden, which in truth represented my heart, my soul, and my hope that life was worth living. While I tended my garden, these plants brought me a degree of innocent happiness as I watched them grow.

My Poor Choice of Vengeance

There was a problem, though: in this vision, my family and other people kept coming down my dirt road, and without provocation and out of pure hate, would absolutely destroy the garden that I loved. I would then go out and carefully re-plant it all, and weeks later, they would come again, ripping everything apart and going on their merry way. I could feel that by enduring this destruction, now I had grown too weary to rebuild the garden of my heart. All I wanted to do now was to seek vengeance against them. I needed to punish them, to make them hurt, to make them bleed. My sense of worthlessness had grown each year, and my anger increased as they destroyed my garden.

I saw myself return to the garden that had been wrecked once again; however, this time, I noticed it had a number of potato size rocks scattered among the crushed plants. I picked up one of the rocks and threw it with all my might down the road, hoping to hit a person or one of my family members and injure them. I wanted revenge because I had not done anything to deserve their continuing, repeated destruction of my heart and soul. I needed them to just leave me alone. The thought of vengeance consumed me, and I stood there throwing rock after rock down the dirt road, even though I knew that they were long past my house. In reality, I was the only person being hurt by throwing these stones of vengefulness.

The Lord's Faithfulness

The Bandals continued to ask me questions, and I told them what I was experiencing so that they could refocus their prayers. As the vision continued, minutes later, I heard the Lord say to me, "Vengeance is mine!" I was startled at first when hearing this. But it wasn't long before I understood in my soul that I was committing a sin by seeking vengeance. It was God's responsibility to take vengeance, and in my heart of hearts, I knew that I had spent years seeking the wrong thing. During the Bandals' prayers, I eventually apologized to God and said, "I am sorry. I am so sorry. It is not my right to seek revenge, Lord. It is yours; Jesus, please forgive me!"

As this vision continued, I saw myself standing still in front of my house. When I lifted my head up and glanced down the road again, I saw hundreds of the rocks that I had thrown at my family and others flying back toward me. I thought, "Oh boy, here comes my punishment. I'm going to get stoned to death for my sins!" Because of my childhood in the Catholic Church, this old thought seemed completely appropriate to me. To protect myself, I turned my back towards the rocks and bent over, instinctively covering my head with my arms. In the next moment, I could hear these large rocks landing all around me and smashing into everything. Oddly enough, I couldn't feel even one of them hitting me. Suddenly, my spirit was hovering twenty feet above my body so that I could observe things unfold without experiencing any pain. It was still a bizarre sensation, but I was grateful that I wouldn't have to suffer the pain of being stoned. I was floating above, watching everything, the house, the garden, and my body, while a shower of rocks came directly at me.

The Lord's Love Is Unsurpassed

Next, I saw the right hand of Jesus totally covering my bent-over body. Oh, the rocks undoubtedly would have hit me if His hand had not been there to protect my body. Once again, Jesus accepted the punishment for sins: my sins of anger, resentment, and vengeance were all falling against the back of His horribly wounded hand. I was even more amazed when I watched these rocks bounce off of Jesus' hand and land in the yard; they were no longer the ugly tan-brown rocks that I had thrown. Each one had been turned into an exquisite stone: bright red rubies, deep green emeralds, diamonds, sapphires, and dark garnets. My yard was filled with every kind of precious stone imaginable, and I could see there was writing in them. My entire front yard and garden had been turned into a sea of dazzling stones, all sparkling in the sunlight. It was an incredibly beautiful and stunning sight to see. Thank you, my Lord, and my God!

Once the barrage of rocks stopped, I floated back into my body. Picking up one of the stones to read what was written in it, my heart broke again with sorrow as it read, "I Love You." "Oh Jesus, I'm so sorry again; You had to be hurt for me to see and get this message." In the other stones, I read things like: "I Am with you always," "You are Forgiven," "Overcomer," "My Beloved," and "My Child." I felt overwhelmed with reverence and was crying as I picked up and read the message inside each of the rocks around me. They had all landed in perfect formation to create a smooth walkway back into the house. Colors were glittering all around creating an awesome sight. Unbelievable! "Jesus, I'm so remorseful that my sins have hurt You again. Please forgive me," I said. In this vision, Jesus once again showed me that when His body covers our sins, the outcome is transformed into something beautiful.

Shortly afterward and unexpectedly, I could hear Jesus softly calling to me from inside my farmhouse. Somehow, I understood that Jesus had been calling to me for years, yearning for me to go back to my house, but I never did. I had been outside stubbornly waiting for the moment when I would have my vengeance. This time, however, I obeyed His call and went up onto my porch and into the house. I opened the wooden screened door and entered an old narrow hallway, which had western-style wood paneling, wooden floor, and tall ceilings. I walked about ten feet down the hallway to my living room off to the left. When I entered this room, my clothing was suddenly changed into a white dress again with lots of lace, almost like a wedding dress. Jesus was standing in the middle of the room with an angel, and to my utter amazement, the room was packed with hundreds of beautifully wrapped gifts that Jesus had wanted to give me for many years. When I was growing up, the teenager within me had yearned to receive these kinds of gifts and blessings from my family. But

I had been stubborn standing outside, throwing rocks, and complaining about not being valued or receiving any blessings. My heart sank as I realized all these things could have been mine earlier if only I had chosen His presence over my need for vengeance. My heart just broke. Again, I said, "Jesus, I am sorry. Please forgive me." Jesus then gave me a tender look of sympathetic understanding, which melted my heart.

Within moments, music began playing, and the angel standing next to Jesus walked up to me and put out His hand. He was very handsome, with brown eyes, brown hair, and dressed in a white robe. His body reflected that He had some kind of authority and experience in battle, but when He looked at me, His gaze was kind, and His touch was tender. He stepped toward me, and we started to slow dance. We danced together for about forty-five seconds, and then Jesus stepped forward and danced with me for a minute or so. I was on cloud nine, just floating in the love that was in that room, the love and tenderness Jesus had for me. My inner child and I truly wanted to remain there and never leave. But the vision slowly faded, and I found myself sitting on the Bandals' couch again.

Prayer Can Cause Change

With their encouragement and prayers, I started the process of forgiving others and releasing the shame that so many of them had burdened me with over the years. I lifted those mentioned above and people in general because the process helped my dignity and self-worth. Thank you, Lord, for loving me and being there with me. There is no way I can ever grasp the totality of Your love for others and me. So I ask, **coincidence or the Hand of God?**

The Bible—A Manual for Living

Jesus had had gifts to give me throughout my entire childhood, but I had not received them because I had been lost in the sins of hatred and vengeance. For it says in Romans 12:19 (ESV), "Beloved, never avenge yourselves, but leave it to the wrath of God, for it is written, 'Vengeance is mine, I will repay, says the Lord.'"

In this paraphrased verse from Revelations 2:17 (NIV), "I will also give to each one who wins the victory a white stone, with a new name written on it. He gave me these stones in the vision, thank you, Lord."

"Make allowance for each other's faults, and forgive anyone who offends you. Remember, the Lord forgave you, so you must forgive others" (Colossians 3:13, NLT). This suggestion might be a difficult one, but my life shows that it's not impossible.

"Be still before the LORD and wait patiently for him; do not fret when people succeed in their ways, when they carry out their wicked schemes" (Psalm 37:7, NIV).

"You turned my wailing into dancing; you removed my sackcloth and clothed me with joy, that my heart may sing your praises and not be silent. LORD my God, I will praise you forever!" (Psalm 30:11–12, NIV).

I'm slowly learning that I cannot change the past, but I *can change my response* to my past. Never pay back evil with more evil. Do things in such a way that everyone can see that you are honorable. Do all that you can to live in peace with everyone. Dear friends, never take revenge. Leave that to the righteous anger of God.

VISION TEN: THE KID ON THE ROOF

Our Spirit Knows

I was still in the Bandals' home, as they kept praying for me to release all my hatred and to find more forgiveness and peace. While they prayed, I suddenly remembered that my mother often told me how she had to call the fire department to get me off the roof of our house. Odd, *Why am I remembering this*, I thought? According to my mother, when I was as young as three years old, I would climb onto the top of the house and sit with my feet dangling off the edge, looking over our backyard. This spot was where I went to often as a child and even into my teens. I can remember feeling an unexplainable compulsion to climb up there. I didn't know why I did it: I just had to! When I climbed up there, my mom wasn't daring enough to climb up after me, and being my father was at work, the only option to get me down was to call the fire department.

Time after time, I climbed the tree by the side of the house, went hand-over-hand along a limb, and dropped down several feet onto the roof. I remembered the fear I felt each time I did it. The roof's slope was moderately steep, and after I had landed, I would slide down a bit, always stopping close to the edge. Getting back down was scarier, though, because I had to jump up and over the edge of the house to grasp the limb I had used to get onto the roof. The steps that I had to take to get onto the roof frighten me even now while I'm remembering it.

At that moment in the Bandals' house, I was surprised that I remembered this habit. I did it the whole time I lived there until I was twelve years old and was kidnapped to go live with my father. I'd seen myself on the roof of the house in my mind's eye hundreds of times over the last twenty to thirty years, but I had no idea why I did it. This behavior never made sense to me, but the Lord was about to explain it.

My Choice

When the vision started, I felt my heart suddenly racing while this strange compulsion began taking control of me. I had to get out of our house, climb that tree, and get on the roof! After I was up there, somehow, I'd feel an unexplainable peace and safety. As the vision continued, I could faintly hear the Bandals praying for the Lord to comfort me because something was seriously compelling me, scaring me to get out of my house. Suddenly, the Lord answered them in a mighty way. The next thing I knew, I was sitting on the roof in the partial shade of our large pecan trees, their mighty limbs swaying in the breeze. I was watching the squirrels play in the yard and feeling the warm roofing shingles under my legs.

The next thing I knew, I saw Jesus walking over to me, and He sat down next to me. He was in a dazzling white robe, wearing sandals, and smiling. He hung His legs over the edge of the roof just like I was doing. After gazing at Him in amazement, I felt tremendous peace, safety, and love flow all over me. Suddenly, it was as if a light bulb, more accurately a *flood lamp*, went off in my head again. Now, I finally understood the calming sensations I felt each time I went up there. Wow, thank you, Jesus. You were always there with me, protecting me. Unexpectedly, out of the corner of my eye, I noticed something moving in our backyard. I was shocked to see a dozen or more evil spirits running back and forth out of the back door of my house, going toward our detached garage in the rear of the property, and then returning into the house. They were running almost right under our feet and moving so fast that I couldn't really see any details about these demons. I could see that they were human-looking, faceless, and dressed in black. I was thinking, *What in the world is going on? What is this?* I remember sitting on the roof dozens of times during my childhood, but I never ever saw anything like this stream of demons before! A few moments after Jesus sat down, all these faceless evil spirits disappeared. It was like something or, I should say correctly, someone had scared them into the next county. They left in a heartbeat, vanishing into thin air! Boom da la boom, they were gone! It seemed as though these less powerful spirits didn't want anything to do with Jesus.

Again, I was faintly aware of the Bandals praying to the

Lord to help me completely forgive my mother! We'd all accepted that this forgiveness process was like the peeling of an onion, layer after layer. As usual, my mind went into a battle of resistance at removing *more deep layers of my resentment.* No, no, no: forgiving her was so incredibly hard. She was the person I had planned to shoot just a few years earlier. Before I could think or say anything, Jesus and I painlessly floated down through the roof of my house. Suddenly, we were standing in the kitchen, side-by-side, facing my mother who was in her wheelchair at the kitchen table. In this part of the vision, I was now maybe twenty-five years old, and my mother was in her 60s. Her gray hair was a mess; her nightgown was thin and torn, and she was sitting in front of an ashtray full of cigarettes. Looking at her face, I saw the all too familiar scow she had when drinking.

Now, however, I was startled to see a six-foot-tall, black demon standing behind her. He looked human and *powerfully built,* about 400 pounds with a shaved head. He was dressed in military gear made of thick leather with metal studs in it. This demon was standing behind my mother and had his left forearm across her forehead, as though he was somehow controlling her mind by the hold he had on her head. He had a staunch look of defiance on his face and was not afraid of Jesus standing there at all!

The Lord's Faithfulness and My Choice

During this part of the vision, another light bulb went off in my head, and I understood the truth about the life I had

had with my mother. During the day when she was sober, she seemed fairly normal, even occasionally nice; for example, some days, she might bring me a hamburger and milkshake for lunch at school. But when she was drunk, she was mean and had lost the ability to function with any kind of morals. I had always thought she was a bit crazy and left it at that. Through this vision, I was allowed to see the reason why she was filled with so much meanness, bigotry, greed, and deceit. I could now begin to understand why she gave me so many nightly beatings and why she would drag me out of bed at midnight in order to watch those documentaries on Hitler. I was now able to understand that she was being horribly controlled. I was grateful for these revelations and insights, but then Jesus looked at me and said, "Do you want me to set her free?" At that moment, I was still reliving my childhood memories. But now! Oh, but now! Now I understood why she had been so cruel and abusive. My eyes started burning with the tears that welled up and ran down my cheeks. Jesus was allowing me to see her tormentor and allowing me to feel true sympathy for my mother. I turned to Jesus timidly and tearfully said, "Yes, set her free!"

Jesus Is Supreme

Jesus then turned his head, looked straight at the demon, and took a step toward him. At the same time, a huge, golden sword appeared in His right hand. Then the demon's armor changed from leather to steel. This demon tightened his hold on my mother's forehead, showing absolutely no fear and complete defiance of Jesus and His authority. Because he was determined to keep hold of his possession, this demon was ready to do battle with Jesus. Jesus lifted His wide golden sword, swung it, and easily cut off the demon's head. Then He made two more slices that cut through the demon's body, but somehow, not harming my mother at all. The demon, however, melted into a black tarry matter surrounding her wheelchair. In the next moment, I saw two angels standing behind us, and Jesus ordered one of them to pick up the tarry mess and bring it to Him on the outside patio behind us. After we had gone out the door, Jesus flung the tarry matter at the right gate of hell, right at the same place where He had imprisoned the demon that had had control over my stepmother. When the black pitch hit the other demon, it acted like hot burning acid, torturing him.

Jesus turned and smiled at me. When He did, pairs of angels all dressed in white appeared and stood guard in front of each door and window in my mother's house. At this point, this vision ended; however, the Lord still had things to reveal to me.

Prayer Changes Things

I never told my mother about all the therapy I had gone through or how much I had hated her, and I never shared any of my visions with her. But within two weeks of this vision, the Lord showed me a *miraculous and mighty change in her and then also in me.* Over the last years of her life, my mother's health declined steadily. She had been drinking bourbon daily since she was sixteen years old, was a chain smoker, and ate very poorly. She had wanted to die at home, and because I was her medical executrix, I had hired nurses' aides to take care of her 24/7. Unfortunately, I had a difficult time keeping caregivers with her because she had such a nasty temperament that she would bite people, throw things, and cuss at the health care workers. As a result, I had to keep hiring new people because no one wanted to keep working with her. Even a group of nuns I had hired quit working with her! *To step on the last nerve of a nun's heart is to say something!* I knew very well that caring for her wasn't a pleasant or easy process.

Within days of her demonic release by Jesus, however, I started getting unbelievable reports. I had begged for some of the aides and nuns who had cared for my mother in the past to return and work with her. They were all stunned and confused by how nice my mother had suddenly become. She was pleasant and kind and grateful to them. *She had totally changed*; she was telling them jokes and showing them photos of places she liked around the world. She would bring out cards and games to play with them. When I heard this, I could hardly believe it. I asked several of the health care workers to tell me again what was happening. My spirit was filled with joy and amazement. Tears filled my eyes as they repeated her story to me again. Jesus, You are beyond words; thank you for her transformation and change. Again, I ask you, **coincidence or the Hand of God?**

The Lord took this remarkable change even further. Two weeks later, He made sure to remove any speck of doubt in my mind concerning His work in her life. To my utter surprise, I received a check from my mother for $26 thousand! For no reason at all! I hadn't said a word to her about money or wanting to get anything. Why should I? She had never given me much of anything. When I saw the check, I fell to my knees in awe and thanksgiving to Jesus. During my teen years, she had hidden away most all the child support money that my father was forced to send her. Prior to this check, she would only send me $20 per year for Christmas. Between all the good reports I was now getting and the check she had sent me, I knew without a doubt Jesus did what He had shown me in the vision. Again, I ask you, **coincidence or the Hand of God?**

Prayer and More Changes

God still wasn't done because He had changed me too. A few months later, I asked Reverend Carmen, my dear pastor and spiritual mother of sorts, to join me when I flew down to Texas to see my mom. After a few days, while we were there, Carmen was able to lead my mother to Christ. Thank you, Jesus! Thank you, thank you! Because of all the work that the Lord had done on my heart regarding my mother, I was given the honor by Carmen to tearfully serve her communion there in the house. She was crying; I was crying; Carmen was crying. What a glorious and tear-filled time, my hands quiver even now upon speaking about it. To experience such unbelievable transformation in both of us, God, you are amazing. Two days later, I gave my mother a surprise birthday party with all the trimmings, including a love song that I wrote and tearfully sang to her. Even while I'm writing this, I can hardly believe these changes happened. Unbelievable! I know that it could only have happened through the immense and tender power of Jesus Christ! To have taken the massive depth of my hatred and somehow turned it into love for my mother! Jesus, Jesus, Jesus! Only you could do this! My mother and I cried and hugged each other for a long time. By the power of Jesus, my heart and hers had been changed, and I knew that the bullet that I had wanted to give her for more than ten years was gone forever. Again, I ask you, **coincidence or the Hand of God?**

The Lord had even more to show me. After I returned to San Diego, a girlfriend of mine named Kris Boggis and I went to a recording studio. While we were there, we made a tape of Christian songs to give my mother, which I mailed along with a tape player. A year later, even though my mother's health was still deteriorating, I decided to go to Europe with four other ladies on a church mission trip. We had developed a two-hour program of songs and testimonies that we shared in three different countries. You guessed it: my testimony was about my mother's deliverance from the demon and the profound changes in both our lives.

More of the Lord's Faithfulness and Wonderment

Our trip included visits to Germany, Austria, and Switzerland. Having grown up with no aunts, uncles, cousins, or grandparents, I didn't know much about where we had come from or my ancestry. I didn't even know the meaning of the word "grandmother" until I was about ten or eleven years old. I was excited about the trip because Austria was the only country that I had ever thought about visiting someday. I had always thought it was because of the movie, *The Sound of Music*, which I loved immensely. But there was something else the Lord was going to show me. Two months before we left, I was surprised to learn that Germany and Austria were two countries of my heritage on my mother's side. And God had arranged that we would present our program in these countries. In addition, we had raised money for the European churches we would visit and brought along Christian tracts to present to each of these churches. Just imagine: here in the countries where the demonic hold on my family probably had its origin, I was now going to present them with money for their churches, tracts, and a testimony of God's transforming love. Wow, again, I ask you, **coincidence or the Hand of God?** *You have to be seeing the hand of God in all of these events by now.*

God Is Not Done with Me Yet

During our seventeen-day tour in Europe, we stayed with church families in their homes. Usually, the five of us shared rooms at two different church homes, but for two nights in a row, I was granted a room by myself, even though I had not asked for it. As it turned out, God was still working on me. From eleven to eighteen years old, I rarely got more than four to five hours of sleep per night. Because of this sleep deprivation, I had made a vow after I graduated from high school that no one would ever disturb my sleep again. Ha, ha! Little did I know that God had other plans for me. So, while I was thrilled to be alone in this room and looking forward to a *long undisturbed night's sleep*, the Lord had other plans. The Lord woke me up both nights, asking me to pray for my mother for two solid hours. *Come on!* My response to His prompting was, "No, no, no. I need my sleep, and I don't want to do this right now." My mind responded very quickly to His request with *Lord, it's the middle of the night!* Silly me, like God didn't know that. Please let me sleep. I had never prayed in the middle of the night for anybody! As much as I struggled to ignore His prodding, I just couldn't. So, I got out from under my down comforter and warm bed, knelt down on the cold floor, and prayed for my mother that night, and you guessed it, the next night, too! I complained to the Lord about it, but it didn't do any good. He even had me get out my journal and write about it the same night. Lord have mercy! I need my sleep!

The Lord Had an Incredible Blessing for Me

After we flew back home to California, I was told that my mother had died and had already been buried in Texas with my brothers' help. When I looked at the date of her passing, I could hardly believe it. It turns out it was the second night that the Lord had gotten me out of my warm, cozy bed with the down blanket to pray on my knees for my mother. Wow, what are the odds that even though I was complaining about being up, the Lord blessed me with being able to pray for my mother during her passing from earth to heaven? Plus, when I contacted the health care workers, they told me that on the morning she died, she had been listening to the tape of Christian music that Kris and I had recorded and sent to her and that she had died peacefully with her arms raised upward.

What were the odds? There had been so many changes: the check she sent me and the amount; she had stopped biting health care aids and started inviting them to join her for a game of cards; her accepting Jesus as her Lord and Savior; my serving her communion, giving her a birthday party that I had never received, and singing her a love song. Then, of all the countries in the world to visit, I went to the country of the origin of the demonic holds on my family, and I went in love with money, tracts, and testimonies of God's transforming love. Plus, while there, He got me out of a warm bed to kneel on a cold floor and pray for two hours, not only *once but twice*. What were the odds of my mother dying while she was listening to the Christian music that I was singing with Kris? Or for her to die peacefully while Jesus had me up praying for her? There is no way this can be seen as anything but the work of the Lord! Amen and amen.

What an awesome God! Never, ever would I have believed He could change two hearts so drastically if I hadn't personally experienced it and seen it with my own eyes. Thank you, Jesus. Thank you, Lord! You are an awesome God, a God beyond words. Again, I ask you, **coincidence or Gods'mighty Hand at work?**

The Bible—A Guide to Living

> Finally, be strong in the Lord and in his mighty power. Put on the full armor of God, so that you can take your stand against the devil's schemes. For our struggle is not against flesh and blood, but against the rulers, against the authorities, against the powers

of this dark world and against the spiritual forces of
evil in the heavenly realms.

Ephesians 6:10–12 (NIV)

This scripture is so incredibly true, and I pray that my story
will help those of you reading it to take heed.

"Having the eyes of your hearts enlightened, that you may
know what is the hope to which he has called you, what are
the riches of his glorious inheritance in the saints" (Ephesians
1:18, ESV).

"The LORD himself goes before you and will be with you;
he will never leave you nor forsake you. Do not be afraid; do
not be discouraged" (Deuteronomy 31:8, NIV).

Put on then, as God's chosen ones, holy and
beloved, compassionate hearts, kindness, humility,
meekness, and patience, bearing with one another
and, if one has a complaint against another, forgiving
each other; as the Lord has forgiven you, so you also
must forgive.

Colossians 3:12–13 (ESV)

Finally, all of you, be like-minded, be sympathetic,
love one another, be compassionate and humble. Do
not repay evil with evil or insult with insult. On the
contrary, repay evil with blessing, because to this you
were called so that you may inherit a blessing.

1 Peter 3:8–9 (NIV)

Wow, what a blessing I received! Jesus will give the same blessing to all those who sincerely seek Him. I have seen undeniable proof that He is with us during our times of trials, fear, and uncertainty. He can cause blessings of the most unexpected type to occur anytime and anywhere. Jesus is Lord of all and most definitely the victor over Satan and his demons. He has the power and willingness to set the captives free. Thank you, Jesus, my Lord, and my God, thank you.

VISION ELEVEN: NEW HOUSE, ROOMS, AND COMMUNION

In October 1997, Gwen had heard of a counselor in the state of Washington by the name of Betty, who was willing to help people walk through the difficulties of forgiveness and shame. Gwen suggested that I visit this lady for counseling; if she had suggested a flight to Germany, I would have gone there, no matter what. I had already come so far, and I needed to complete this journey of forgiveness.

Support Is Out There

I took Gwen's suggestion and flew up to Washington. For a week, I met daily for six hours with Betty, who was another holy woman of God. I had the most beautiful and profound vision thus far when I was with her. Every day when I arrived at Betty's home, I felt that God sent a flock of birds to greet me. Betty had a small bush right next to her sidewalk, and every day, there were thirty or more sparrows on it, just chirping their little heads off as to welcome me. As soon as I reached the bush, they would all jump inside and become quiet, and when I had passed, they would all come back out and chirp with all their might. Somehow, and I know it is odd, but this flock of sparrows gave me a sense that someone was watching over me.

My Choice to Finish Cleaning My Soul

Betty gave me homework every night, and we spent a good portion of each session in prayer. We were in the process of peeling away deeper layers of my anger. On Saturday, Betty and I entered into intense prayer, and after almost two hours, I had another vision. I was standing outside an old-fashioned wooden farmhouse, the type you would see driving along a country road. I saw Jesus and a nine-year-old me sitting just outside my farmhouse on a bench. I could feel that it was my home, even though it didn't look anything like the house where I had grown up in Texas.

Over the years that I had been doing my work on forgiveness, I had often felt like I was cleaning a house, a house in my soul. I had been going from room to room, and at this point, I had only one room left in my soul's house to clean. But I was absolutely terrified to enter it. I had a feeling that there was a demon standing just inside the door. And I was certain that if I went in there, he would grab me and pull me inside the room against my will, and I would die. I'm embarrassed to say this, that even after all that the Lord had shown me, I still had an irrational fear of this room in my soul. Betty first focused her prayers on courage so that I would have the courage that I needed to enter this room.

My Hardest Choice—Letting God Lead Me

Even though Jesus was there, and even after everything I'd seen, everything He had shown me, everything He had done to protect me, I knew that it was going to take all the courage I could muster to enter that last room. It is not easy for human nature to give up control. But God says we are *not* to live worldly lives, but to live for Christ and bear witness of His truth to the world. I could faintly hear Betty say to me to "Seek Him; He will save you. Live for Him; He will open up heaven's door for you." So, I lifted up a small prayer asking Jesus to help me. Then Jesus and I stood up, and we went up the stairs onto the front porch and entered the house. After walking a few feet down a hallway, we went into the first doorway to the right. I was blown over and astounded to see a beautiful, crystal-clear pond right in front of us. There was a waterfall feeding into the pond from a lush green mountain. The mountain and the pond were beautiful, pristine, so clean, so fresh and new as if they had just been created. The overwhelming beauty took my breath away. Jesus then took me by the hand, and we walked into the pond until it was up to our shoulders. The temperature was perfect, not too cold and not too warm. There was a fine mist all around the waterfall, and the sun's light was creating rainbows that danced all around us. What a glorious, glorious sight! Thank you, Lord, this is incredible!

Even though the setting was amazing, I was wondering why He had brought me down into the water. In answer to my own question, I got the feeling that I needed to be cleansed of the spirits of fear and rejection, and this incredible pond was somehow a part of it. As Jesus had told His disciples: if the people in a town do not accept you and your words, then dust off your sandals and never return. Jesus had told me in my second vision that even though my family hadn't really wanted me, heaven had watched over me since I was a baby. We stayed in the pond for only a minute or two, and then Jesus led me back out. We again opened the door and entered the hallway, and immediately we were absolutely dry, clothes and all. *Jesus, this is just so cool!*

Jesus continued to lead me down the hallway until we came to a second door. We stepped in, and there were lush green mountains in front of us. These powerful and majestic mountains spanned from west to east and had a river flowing at the bottom. They reminded me of mountains that I had seen on one of the islands of Hawaii or New Zealand. The numerous peaks were totally covered in lush vegetation; each mountain jutted out toward the winding river and then retreated, creating a zigzag pattern. There was unbelievable newness and unspoiled beauty everywhere, like an amazing paradise. The mountains extended on and on as far as I could see. *Oh, Lord, this is so beautiful,* I thought. *How magnificent are your works! How glorious are your creations, Father!*

After a few minutes of contemplation, Jesus led me down the hallway again into the third room. As soon as we took one step inside, we were on top of the world's tallest mountain. Don't ask me how I knew that, but I did. We could see for a hundred miles, looking over mountain range after mountain range. All the mountains were covered in snow, the sky was crystal blue, and of course, the sun was shining. The mountains glistened and shimmered like they had been sprinkled with diamonds and glitter. So many colors! We were standing on a snowy peak, and amazingly I couldn't feel the chill of this winter wonderland. We were perfectly comfortable. *Jesus, you think of everything; oh my goodness!* Everything was so fresh that I felt as if God created all of this beauty just for us. So new, beautiful, powerful, and majestic! I only wish I had words to explain how inexplicably magnificent this sight was. We stood there for a minute or so and then exited that room. We turned, walked back into the hall the way we had just come, and entered a doorway on our right. After we walked inside, I didn't know whether we grew larger or if the universe became smaller, but all of a sudden, we were standing in front of Saturn. Yes, the planet Saturn! Dear Lord! After I caught my breath at the sight, I reached out with my right hand and touched Saturn's spinning red, orange, and yellow dust rings. I pulled my hand back and forth several times like a kid playing with a new fascinating and mesmerizing toy. It was so beautiful and fun seeing all the colors getting mixed up by my hand. I still don't know whether Saturn became smaller or if we had supernaturally enlarged, but it was a blast. Jesus, this is so incredible and beautiful, thank you. As with the other rooms, we only stayed a minute or two, then we left.

More of the Lord's Awesomeness

Jesus led me to the fifth and final room. Not surprisingly, the awesome wonder that I had been feeling in the other rooms made me completely forget my earlier fears; they were nowhere to be found! I was absolutely flooded with joy, amazement, wonder, thankfulness, and loving peacefulness. Wow, oh wow. Then He opened the last door, and I saw a long white banquet room, and not a single demon was anywhere in sight. Hallelujah! An elongated wooden table was arranged in the middle of the room, and there were a number of people in the chairs along each side. When I looked more closely at the guests, I realized that they were ten generations of my family. I also saw two angels dressed in white in the room. Jesus took me and sat me down at the near end of the table, and then He walked down to the other end. While He stood there, I noticed that there was a large, round loaf of bread and a chalice in front of Him. He took the loaf, lifted it up, broke it in half, and said to everyone there, "This is my body broken and given for you. Take of it in remembrance of me." Then He handed one half of the loaf to each side of the table. Next, He lifted the chalice in front of Him and said, "This is my blood given for you. Drink of it in remembrance of me."

He handed a chalice to each side of the table, and I watched as the first person partook of the bread and wine. Each family member then turned to the next generation, their offspring who were sitting next to them, and asked them for forgiveness of something they had passed down through the generations. I could not hear what each person was saying, but I could understand that each person was asking for forgiveness. After each offspring had forgiven his or her parent, each would partake of the bread and wine. Then he or she would repeat the process with the next generation and ask forgiveness for passing down some sort of sin to them. This happened in each of the generations on both sides of the table. I never learned which generation introduced the demonic presence into the family line, but as the scene continued, each person forgave or was forgiven and started crying. They all partook of the elements and passed them down toward the end of the table where I was seated.

Eventually, all twenty people finished, and I looked down at the two halves of bread passed to me. But they had become one whole round loaf again. My mind was puzzled; *How could that be after twenty people had just partaken of the bread?* I thought. *How could it be one loaf of bread again?* I was amazed and confused. Then Jesus walked around to my end of the table and stood facing me. I was still sitting in the chair when He tore off a piece of the bread, dipped it into the wine, and offered it to me. I stood up and partook of it with tears flowing down my cheeks. I then offered Him a big hug, so He knelt down to be at eye level with my nine-year-old self. I looked at His loving eyes and then kissed Him on His left cheek and noticed how incredibly soft His beard was. My mind was in a misty wonderment at all I had just experienced and seen.

It was beyond words to truly describe the majesty of it all. I was speechless while I hugged Him, and somehow, I knew of His tremendous love and forgiveness of each person there. The vision slowly ended with the warmth and tenderness of the Father's love being poured over my entire body.

Every cell in my body knew something unbelievable had just happened. I had seen ten generations of my family confess their sins to each other, and every one of them had been forgiven. I truly, truly believe something miraculous, something holy and sacred, happened to the other people in that vision. I guess I'll have to wait until I'm in heaven to know what became of all that I'd been shown and experienced.

This vision happened on the last day of my week with Betty; once we were done, she walked me to my car. As we passed her rose garden, without asking me, Betty went over, cut a flower off, and gave it to me. It was the only rose left as the winter season had arrived. Looking at it, I realized that it was just like the rose Jesus had given me in my second vision. I was shocked that the bush was still flowering because it was so late in the year. In fact, the very next week, it snowed. At the same time, I felt as if Jesus wanted to give me something tangible to hold in my hand to represent His love. Thank you, my Lord and my God. You deserve all praise and worship!

The Lord truly blessed me by giving me two holy and spiritual moms: Reverend Carmen Warner Robbins and Gwen Hurst, and a remarkable and faithful friend like Lynn Bailey. I don't think that I would have made it to the Lord's banquet table without them. I know I will never be able to repay all the wonderful men and women who have prayed for me, but

I know that God will repay them. The angels in heaven are dancing because these godly prayer warriors asked Jesus to help me forgive multiple generations of my family and ancestors. Thank you, Jesus! Lord of all, Master and King of everything seen and unseen, You are truly the most Holy One! You are our Healer, Redeemer, and loving Father. This You share with all who will believe in and accept You as their Lord and Savior. Oh, I can hardly wait to spend eternity with You! Jesus, You are the Alpha and the Omega, the first and the last, the beginning and the end. Jesus, You're the advocate for our terrible sins, and You paid for all of them! Thank you for being our Deliverer from the wages of our sins and freeing us from the wrath to come to those who won't accept You. Jesus, You are our great High Priest, sitting at God's right hand. When we see Gods' beauty in creation all around us, may we be reminded to lift our heads and give Him praise and glory? If we humbly bring Jesus the scars of our damaged past, He can heal us. He knows the truth of why the people in our family reacted to life the way they did. He alone knows how to treat the festering and painful wounds so that the injuries left by them are finally healed. Today as you read this, it is the time to acknowledge your sins before Jesus and accept His healing and merciful love for you. Don't turn away! Tomorrow is not promised to anyone; He is there and awaiting your simple prayer of help. Thank you, Lord.

The Bible—Love Instructions Given by Our Lord

"If we confess our sins, he is faithful and just to forgive us our sins and to cleanse us from all unrighteousness" (1 John

1:9, ESV).

As Deuteronomy affirms below, when a person turns back to God in obedience, He showers that person with His steadfast love. That love contains a promise of complete healing for that person and all the generations of that person's family through the ministry of our Lord Jesus Christ.

> You shall not make for yourself a carved image, or any likeness of anything that is in heaven above, or that is on the earth beneath, or that is in the water under the earth. You shall not bow down to them or serve them; for I the LORD your God am a jealous God, visiting the iniquity of the fathers on the children to the third and fourth generation of those who hate me, *but showing steadfast love to thousands of those who love me and keep my commandments.*
>
> Deuteronomy 5:8–10 (ESV)

"This is what the Scriptures mean when they say, 'No eye has seen, no ear has heard, and no mind has imagined what God has prepared for those who love him'" (1 Corinthians 2:9, NLT). I can hardly wait to see heaven.

"The heavens declare the glory of God, and the sky above proclaims his handiwork" (Psalm 19:1, ESV). I truly believe that creation is the canvas of God's character.

"You prepare a table before me in the presence of my enemies. You anoint my head with oil; my cup overflows" (Psalm 23:5, NIV). Thank you, Lord.

I was so terrified a demon was waiting for me in that house.

Oh, how wrong I was! Thank you, Jesus. "I sought the LORD, and he answered me; he delivered me from all my fears" (Psalm 34:4, NIV).

"In his hand are the depths of the earth, and the mountain peaks belong to him" (Psalm 95:4, NIV). Big and unbelievably glorious ones at that!

"He brought me to the banquet hall, and he looked on me with love" (Song of Solomon 2:4, HCSB). We are significant, not because of what we do but because of who we are. What makes us special is the signature of God in our lives. With God, you aren't an accident or mistake: you are a gift to the world, a divine work of art signed by God Himself. An original masterpiece that is priceless!

"Call to Me, and I will answer you, and show you great and mighty things, which you do not know" (Jeremiah 33:3, NKJV). Everything I saw was great and mighty and unbelievably beautiful. Thank you, my Lord, and my God!

THE MIRACLE OF A NEW JOB

Going back in time, I'm going to share with you a series of mini-miracles in 1989 that the Lord gave me *before* I began to trust Him at all. These events happened after my sister committed suicide and I had divorced my alcoholic husband of ten years. These two events compounded years of built-up anger and hatred I had stored up at humankind and my family. My years of struggling with depression hit an all-time high. I was losing my ability to handle anything in my life. As I stated, it was 1989, and I was suicidal again and just wanted to join my sister in death. I thought about turning to my parents for comfort, but they were both alcoholics and the biggest source of the anger that fueled my depression.

I had been working as a registered nurse in critical care for ten years. Then one day, I mentally crashed. I had been assigned to a seventy-five-year-old woman who needed surgery because she had fallen down drunk at home and fractured her hip. Instead of being eager to have the surgery and begin healing, she was more determined to return home and resume her drinking, no matter what. When I entered her room, I found her struggling to crawl out of her bed. I certainly didn't want her to fall again and injure her hip even more. In an attempt to get her flailing arms and leg back in bed, I tried everything and eventually had to literally lie across her abdomen. While I was holding her down, she started beating, screaming, and spitting at me, struggling the entire time to get up, go home, and drink. Because she had tossed her call button on the floor, I eventually had to shout for help. Within moments, another nurse came in and got some restraints to secure the patient safely in bed. Lesson learned: don't underestimate the strength of a seventy-five-year-old!

The woman was a chronic alcoholic, and I knew that it was my job to protect this patient from further harming herself. However, something inside me snapped. I had spent years receiving that type of treatment from the alcoholics in my life. I had reached my emotional breaking point, and I decided that it would be the last day that I worked in critical care. I called my current therapist and had her call my boss and inform her that I would not be returning to work. My therapist then had me immediately admitted into a treatment facility near Phoenix, Arizona. I was deeply depressed and was experiencing homicidal and suicidal thoughts; everything in me had reached a boiling point. I felt that something was going to give, or someone was going to die.

I knew deep inside that if I got out of the treatment center in Arizona, I could not return to my prior position. I discerned I could never work so intimately with patients again, so just prior to leaving for Arizona, I applied for a different job as an operating room nurse. I was in the worst possible frame of mind to handle an interview, but I didn't care. In fact, I had spent forty-five minutes just that morning staring into my closet trying to decide what I would wear, when on most days, I would just grab some clothes and go. My mind was on overload and going into a permanent, ugly downward spiral. The interviewer, who was the chief nurse of the department, told me that because there was a shortage of operating room nurses, they wanted to start a training program. I told her that I was interested but that I had to go *somewhere* for a while and didn't know when I'd return. Miraculously, she was okay with my vague answer, and *some nine months later*, she remembered me and was eager that I start the training program for the job. *Hmm, how did that happen?* It was just one of a number of mini-miracles God had planned for me.

In Arizona, I was admitted to an inpatient facility for six weeks. The staff invited both of my parents to attend a family-week session. However, my mother couldn't come because of her continuous drinking, and my father declined, saying that he was building a custom home and didn't have the money. I felt that his rejection was another low blow. His oldest daughter had just committed suicide, and now his only living daughter had been admitted for wanting the same option, but he couldn't afford to come. The truth was that he was on his third marriage and needed to impress his wife financially. That they were in the process of building a custom home. The $1,500 it would have cost to come was just too much to spend on his daughter. Interesting, even all the drug addicts and ex-cons in my group were able to have some relative come for the family sessions. I was hurt deeply and ashamed that I was the only one on whom neither parent could invest even a moment of time in my life.

Then I received my second mini-miracle, a therapist with the same name as my deceased sister. With all the therapists in the facility, how was it I was assigned to her? The wound in my heart of my sister's death and my feelings of abandonment, pain, and shame were now getting reopened. I could still remember the week that I spent cleaning my sister's apartment, fighting off the flies and the maggots that were feasting on her bloody carpet. I really didn't want to remember that time in my life or that sight! When my sister died, I lost the main person I could share my feelings with and the family member I could really lean on to help me.

After four weeks of treatments, my depression only worsened. The treatment facility transferred me then to a hospital in Phoenix for ECT (electroshock treatments), and I was assigned a personal suicide watcher 24/7. Then the ECT treatments started the very next day. God's third mini-miracle was that I only received four out of the six ECT's that had been scheduled for me. After the first treatment, I was left with excruciating soreness in every muscle, and I had soiled myself. After laying in the bed for six hours and smelling the mess in my underwear, knowing that the nursing staff hadn't even bothered to clean me up or give me any pain medication only increased my anger. Weeks later, before my fifth treatment, someone from the hospital business center came into my padded cell and informed me that my insurance had lapsed and I was going to be discharged immediately. I'm sorry to say that they didn't waste any time either, because the next thing I knew, I was standing in the parking lot, looking at my car keys and wondering what to do with them. The ECT had worked for me; it had broken my depression by breaking my entire emotional center: it was a very odd sensation because I didn't feel anything, good or bad, happy or sad. I also felt as if my brain had been scrambled, and it had been. As it turned out, receiving only four out of the planned six ECT treatments was a blessing in disguise.

The fourth mini-miracle from God occurred when I got into my car. I had to sit there for some time, trying to remember how to drive a stick shift. Plus, I had to use the old-fashioned paper maps to try and find my way home to San Diego. Dear Lord, help me! I got on the road and then had to think long and hard concerning what a green traffic light versus a red light meant. Everything about driving was now a slow mental effort. I was shocked at how bad my memory was. This added for some close calls! I truly don't know how I got home, but I do know that the grace of God guided me. To this day, I have no memory of driving home or of the two months that followed my return to San Diego.

Eventually, I called my medical insurance carrier, and the service representative informed me that the Arizona hospital had made a mistake. I still had more medical coverage. I now believe this was God's way of saving some of my brain's function by limiting the number of ECT treatments that I had received. Thank you, Lord.

By this time, five to six months had passed since I had interviewed for that new job as an operating room nurse. I went back to my hospital, and the chief nurse miraculously remembered me and said she had been wondering where I had gone. I evaded her question and told her that I still needed *more time* before I started the new job. By some miracle, she agreed to it. Wow! Another God moment! After another three months, I returned to work and started the training. Even after that much time, I probably came back to work too soon because I was still experiencing lapses in my memory. But I had run out of money, so off to training I went. Thanking God for the memories I did retain.

Because the training program was brand new, I was the first and only nurse that the OR staff had to train. To say that this absolutely new training program did not go smoothly is putting it lightly. Two weeks after I started in the operating room, the nurse who was assigned to train me got fired. This was in large part due to a written report that two other nurses and I gave to the chief nurse about the treatment/training program she had for me. The firing happened quickly: two hours after the chief nurse read our reports, my assigned training nurse was fired and escorted off the property. My training nurse had worked in that facility for more than twenty years, and she had a number of friends who were now upset with me and took little time making it known to me just how they felt. Because I was involved in her losing her job, I experienced horrible feelings of guilt. In addition, two weeks after that firing, the chief nurse who had hired me and started the whole training program was fired too! The training program and I were now floundering, to put it lightly! Many of the OR staff really did not want the extra work or responsibility of training me. The few who did train me made working there much, much harder than necessary.

Once again, God stepped in with another mini-miracle. After a couple of months in the OR, I received a written notice of pending termination due to poor performance. This was not a surprise since almost no one was training me. This put me in a pure panic state; if I lost my job, I'd lose my home. My nerves were unraveling, and tears were like a waterfall. But then, at the last minute, a Christian nurse named Anna Suazo stepped up and said that she would personally take over my entire training program. To this day, she has a special place in my heart for saving my job, my career, and my sanity. The training took an extra three months, lasting nine months in all, but it was well worth it. She was a great, kind, and gentle teacher, and I will eternally love her.

I experienced another mini-miracle some months after my training was completed. I had already functioned as an OR scrub nurse a couple of times with one of the most demanding but technically talented surgeons in the OR. He was known for not having any patience for anything except perfection, and he would loudly let everyone know if a nurse didn't measure up, management included. I was frightened to death of him, and I tried never to be assigned to his cases. In fact, I was so scared of working in the OR that I'd practically be sick every morning. I developed a habit prior to going into work of sitting in my car every morning and crying. I was trying to build up my nerve to enter the building. One day though, I decided to try what Carmen and Gwen had recommended for me: *pray before doing anything*. So, I sat there in my car and gave it a try; I started praying intensely, asking God to surround me with pleasant and pleasurable people in the operating room and help me to do my very best.

Later that day, I got assigned to the above very demanding surgeon. Go figure! Plus, he was going to do a very technically intense and difficult surgery, which I had minimum experience with thus far. In my tiny, prayerful heart, I cried out, "Oh, dear Lord, just kill me now!" I immediately ran into the bathroom crying, asking God why? I had prayed! And I had asked Him for pleasant people and easy cases. I was angry: why had God let me down? After a few minutes of crying to the Lord, I heard the words, "Trust me!" It was so profound that it shocked me, and I stopped crying immediately! Puzzled by hearing this, I gathered up all the nerve I had and got ready for a very intense and difficult case.

The surgery started, and I was elbow to elbow with this surgeon, assisting with the case. To my surprise, everything was going great! This surgeon, who actually had legal court cases against him because of his attitude toward nurses in surgery, was now laughing and joking around with me. I was on pins and needles, waiting for the bubble to pop and for him to chew me up and spit me out of his room. The case went on for more than two hours, and he could not have been nicer. I was dumbfounded! How was it possible? Eventually, a relief nurse came to take over my case so that I could go to lunch. While I was walking out of the OR, the surgeon even said "Goodbye" to me and was still smiling and pleasant. I thought that I was dreaming. The nurse who took over my case had more years of experience than I did, so I was confident that there wouldn't be any kind of a problem with her as his scrub nurse.

I had been out of the OR maybe three minutes when the nurse who had relieved me came into the lounge where I was. *She shouldn't be here.* I thought, *She just took over my case.* The next thing I knew, she was cussing and slamming her locker.

She was very upset about something. I asked her what was wrong, and she told me that she had just been chewed up and spit out by this same surgeon. I couldn't believe my ears: he had been so nice to me all morning, me a newbie. Here she was, a much more qualified nurse, and for some reason, he had turned on her. He had been a cream puff for me during my time in the OR with him.

She kept cussing, and I had to sit down because my legs started shaking. I didn't share with her how nice he had been with me all morning. While I might have lacked some training, I was not stupid enough to make a bad situation even worse. If I told her how nice he had been with me, I truly think she would have hit me! Then, I suddenly remembered the words the Lord gave me while I was crying in the bathroom earlier. "Trust me!" Wow, oh wow! Maybe this prayer stuff works! There simply wasn't another explanation. That surgeon had never been nice to me until that day.

Later that day, I finished another surgery and helped the anesthesiologist take a patient to the recovery room as usual. While I was leaving the recovery room, I noticed that one of the other patients had "coded," meaning that their heart had stopped. There were already a number of nurses and doctors working on the patient, trying to revive them. So, I went about my business and headed back to the OR, but on the way, I felt an unusually strong desire to pray for that patient and the code team. I stepped around the corner of the recovery room so that no one would see me. I did not have any idea who they were, but I felt strangely compelled to pray for them. This was so odd and out of place for me. But I did pray, "Lord, if it is time for this person to die, please forgive them of any sins, wash them clean with the blood of Jesus, and welcome them into heaven." I also asked the Lord to help the code team to revive them. It wasn't a long prayer, but when it ended, I felt an unraveling presence of a large, male person dancing all around me. The feeling was so strong that I could have joined in with the dancing. Because I was still fairly new to prayer, I must admit that the feeling of this spirit's presence scared the wahoos out of me! I'd never had anything like that happen before. I left the recovery room in a really big hurry! Later that day, I found out that it was a large man who had coded and that he had died. It left chills up and down my arms. Thank you, Jesus, for the urge to pray and also for the dancing spirit around me. So, I ask, were all these **coincidences or the Hand of God?**

How is it that all these things happened? The Lord had given me a therapist with my sister's name so that my hidden wounds concerning her death would be opened and healed. He cut the ECT therapy short to help save some of my brainpower. He guided me home from Arizona, even when I hardly knew the difference between a green light and a red one or the clutch from the brake. Then the Lord knew I needed a new job, and He pulled out all the stops to make sure I got one, holding a job open for me for nine months. Then He gave me an understanding Christian nurse to complete my training, just when I was about to be fired. I eventually excelled in the OR for sixteen years until my feet gave out, and I had to look for another position. Then He also gave me the opportunity to pray for a stranger in his last seconds on earth before dying. The Bible was helping me see that God warns us not to wait until the last minute to ask for forgiveness. For no one knows what the future holds; life is uncertain. Death can snatch us before we even have time to cry out to the Lord. Even in the darkest moment, God is willing to shed light into the darkness. He had shown me how powerful prayer could have an influence on myself and on others. Jesus is the only One who really knows where your life here is going. No matter what your plans are, no matter your own will, His ways are always better, and His pathway will lead you to the glories He has in store for each of us. Don't trust your feelings; trust only in God's Word. He created everything we know and see and touch; shouldn't He know how things are supposed to work. He left us an instruction manual for a bountiful life called the Bible. Wow, what a God we have! So, when I was led to read the following scriptures, it sent chills up my arms.

'For I know the plans I have for you,' declares the LORD, 'plans to prosper you and not to harm you, plans to give you hope and a future. Then you will call on me and come and pray to me, and I will listen to you. You will seek me and find me when you seek me with all your heart.'

Jeremiah 29:11–13 (NIV)

"The LORD is a refuge for the oppressed, a stronghold in times of trouble. Those who know your name trust in you, for you, LORD, have never forsaken those who seek you" (Psalm 9:9–10, NIV).

"Trust in the LORD with all your heart, and do not lean

on your own understanding. In all your ways acknowledge him, and he will make straight your paths" (Proverbs 3:5–6, ESV). We cannot fathom the things the Lord can and will do for us if we have faith in Him. He is an awesome God!

THE MIRACLE OF THE MYSTERIOUS BOOK

This next miracle still blows me away when I think about it! It happened around October 1998 when a special Christian girlfriend of mine, Dana Erwin, picked up a couple of books that someone at her work was giving away. It was just a collection of odds and ends, but she took a couple of them, handing me one at church the next Sunday.

I must be honest: I am not a reader. The problem is that I am dyslexic, and my reading and writing skills are only moderate. I've read plenty of medical books, but that's about it. I have only read four or five short novels in my life. My childhood was spent in sports, not reading. I did read several self-help books trying to get through my battle with depression and co-dependency, but basically, I'm not a reader. I thanked Dana for the book and tossed it on a bookshelf at home. It seems funny that I call it a "bookshelf" because the shelf hardly has any books on it. It collects more nick-knacks than books.

During the two years before I received this book, I had primarily been working on my need to forgive my family members. I really didn't believe in the demonic before I started receiving my visions, but because several of the visions involved the demonic, my mind was eventually changed. This understanding led to an intense interest in what was going on behind the scenes with me, my family, and my ancestry. On one of my visits to Texas, I talked with a Christian lady friend of my mother's. She had known my mom since childhood. Somehow, we began talking about the subject of the demonic. She then told me that she truly thought that either my grandmother or great-grandmother dabbled in witchcraft or possibly was a witch. *Wow*, I thought, *maybe there is something about the demonic and generational sin I had read about in the Bible.*

When I returned to San Diego, I spoke to Dana and other Christian friends, and most of them believed in generational sins and curses. I was becoming more interested in the subject, and when I walked past my bookshelf, I noticed the book Dana had given me almost a year earlier. The title of the book was *Healing The Family Tree* by Dr. Kenneth McAll. *Hmm, that's fascinating*, I thought and spent the next week reading it. He was talking about how generational sins can be passed down through the family line, and he was also quoting statements from other authors who had written on the same subject.

Feeling fatigued from reading, I got up from my kitchen table and walked into the living room. On my footstool, I noticed a book sitting all alone, which was a very rare event in my house! I went over to see what it was about and nearly had a heart attack. It was one of the *other books* that Dr. Kenneth

McAll was talking about in his book. Holy, holy, holy, where did that book come from? I was scared to touch it. I couldn't believe my eyes. I must say: it sent shivers up my spine. The book was *From Generation To Generation* by Patricia Smith. So, I went back to McAll's book to double-check the title, and yes, it *was* one of the books he quoted. Even to this day, I don't know how it got into my house. After I finally worked up the courage to touch it, I began to read it too. It confirmed that there is a phenomenon of passing down generational curses. I approached my spiritual mom Gwen, about all of this, and she assured me there are generational sins and curses. She then gave me the name of a lady to call who had another book on the same subject in her collection. The book was entitled *Healing Your Family Tree* by a priest, Father John Hampsch, from Los Angeles.

I buried myself in that book as well. Because I wanted Gwen and my pastor to read the first two books, I tried unsuccessfully to find them in my local bookstores. In the end, I loaned my copies of the books to Gwen and my pastor. At that time, most people still used the Yellow Pages to locate stores. So, I pulled out mine and started calling every bookstore in San Diego because I wanted another copy of Patricia's book. I wanted a new, physical copy because; options for reading it on a cell phone or computer were not available. Because San Diego is a city of over a million people, it had a large number of bookstores. I spent all day calling numbers from the Yellow Pages, and I did not find any store that had or could even order Patricia Smith's book. Where in the world had my copy come from? I called the very last store, which was a tiny mom-and-pop shop. An elderly gentleman answered the phone, and I told him the title that I needed. Without covering the phone, he hollered in a shaky voice to his wife, "Myrtle, do we have a copy of *From Generation to Generation?*" I was thinking to myself, *This is useless.* All of a sudden, his wife hollered back, "No! But I think a lady named Barbara McBride might have one." I wrote the name down, scratched my head, and hung up.

Strangely enough, I had known a Barbara McBride from years earlier, but I couldn't believe that it could be the same person. What are the odds that when someone says a name from the million-plus residents of your city, it would be someone you know? I was willing to give it a shot, though, so I looked around the house for my address book. Eventually, I found it buried under something and got her number. Feeling like a fool, I called Miss Barbara about Patricia's book. To my complete amazement, she had several copies of it. What are the odds again? I ask you, **coincidence or the Hand of God?**

While I was speaking to Barbara, she said she knew the author personally and that Patricia was coming to San Diego for a church conference. I also discovered that Barbara only lived five or six blocks from me. Goodness, another "wow" moment! She invited me over, and I purchased several additional copies of Patricia's book. The story doesn't end here. No, God had a few more "wow" moments for me. A couple of weeks had passed when Barbara called to say that Patricia was in town and at her house. She asked if I wanted to meet her and, if so, to come on over. Well, I jumped at the chance to talk to this author in person. She was a very gentle and loving person who was more than willing to talk with me, and she even ended up praying over me. I thanked her and went back home feeling very blessed and in awe that I had met the author.

Around the same time, I had been attending an annual, weeklong prayer and healing camp east of Los Angeles. I had plans to attend it again that year, and I did go later in the same month that I met Patricia. The camp had a maximum capacity of 200 people. The first evening we sat in the dinner hall at round tables that each held ten people. I randomly sat down at one and noticed Gwen, my spiritual mom, was sitting right across from me. I was pleased to see her at the camp because I had grown very fond of her and was glad she'd be here all week. While I was sitting there, Gwen started making a head motion for me to notice the person who was sitting on my right. He was a very elderly gentleman, but I had no idea who he was. Gwen was grinning from ear to ear and couldn't contain herself. So, she came over and whispered in my ear, "Don't you know him?" When I replied that I didn't, she continued, "That gentleman is Dr. Kenneth McAll, the author of that book you loaned me." The Prayer and Healing Conference had flown him from England to be the main speaker for the entire weeklong retreat. Again *Holy, holy, holy*, I thought. *Wow, he is right next to me.* Because Dr. McAll was quite elderly and I was a registered nurse, I took it upon myself to walk him to his cabin each night after dinner. What a blessing it was to introduce myself and talk with him about his work!

Before I left San Diego for this retreat, I had written to the priest in Los Angeles who had written *Healing Your Family Tree*. I had asked him if I could have a one-on-one prayer session with him. After I returned home, he called and stated that he was just too busy to do a lengthy one-on-one, but he did pray with me over the phone and said a mass for me.

My experiences with these books were true miracles. I hadn't asked to receive any of these books, and I even managed to read all three of them in less than three months! Then I actually got to speak with all three authors and meet two of them in person. To me, it's beyond coincidence. So, I ask you, **coincidence or the Hand of God?**

THE MIRACLE ON THE ROAD

In 2002, God did a miracle for my husband and me when we were heading back home to San Diego after visiting friends in the city of Carlsbad. We'd left their home after sunset on a Sunday night, and a thick fog had started moving in from the Pacific Ocean. The traffic was moderately heavy while we were coming down Interstate 5 along the coast. At that time, the freeway had five southbound lanes, and we were driving in the second fast lane from the left. My husband was driving, and I was about to fall asleep. We were going sixty-five to seventy mph when, all of a sudden, we both heard tires screeching like they were right on top of us. Well, they were! In the next second, we were hit on the rear driver's side by another car, which took out that left door area. The next thing we knew, we were in a full spin to the left, heading eastward toward the concrete freeway barrier that divided the southbound traffic from the northbound. After we had spun one and a half times, I looked out my passenger window and saw the concrete barrier outside my door. We were about to crash into it, and I knew that my head was going to hit the door's window and shatter it. So, I quickly closed my eyes, hoping not to get glass in them. Another second or so passed, but miraculously, we didn't crash into the barrier. We were still spinning, but somehow the car was now moving to the west back across the freeway, in exactly 180 degrees opposite the direction that we had been traveling. I looked up, and all I could see were car headlights coming toward us.

Because I was a Christian, I probably should have instinctively yelled Jesus' name or a prayer, but I didn't. I did speak, but my first instinct was to reassure my husband. "Hun, you're doing great!" I told him. Then I looked more closely at him, and I could see that he wasn't doing anything except putting a death grip on the steering wheel. He had not turned the wheel at all. The spins continued, and I had a second chance to call on the Lord for help. But no, while the approaching headlights got closer, I told my husband, "You're still doing great, Hun!" Goodness, where was all my Christian teaching, yelling out to my husband instead of God! Wow, this is embarrassing to even write. I wonder if I should erase this part. Ugh! Sorry, God!

We spun three times heading west and ended up facing south on the freeway, in the second to the slowest lane from the right. We could see the car that had hit us was in the lane in front of us, so we followed it to the shoulder of the freeway.

Because there was freeway construction all around us, the concrete barriers were up to the edge on the right side of the freeway. We surprisingly found one small turnout a little ahead of us, and luckily enough, both of our cars just managed to fit in it. I looked over at my husband, and he seemed fine, although he still had a death grip on the wheel. When we came to a stop, I had to wait for my adrenaline-infused legs to stop bouncing up and down again. They do that from time to time when my life flashes before my eyes. Because the traffic was rushing by the car a foot or two away, my husband couldn't open his door, so I got out of the car to check on the other driver. The young girl was shaken up but physically fine. We needed to call for help, but none of us owned a cell phone. It looked like we were going to sit in our cars until someone arrived to help us or until the morning light! I wouldn't even consider having someone trying to get us help by walking along the freeway at night in the fog with no freeway shoulder available. I must say it was unnerving to sit in the car while it shook from side to side as each car or truck sped by.

But again, the Lord provided. Just for a second, the fog broke, and I noticed an emergency call box five feet or so in front of the other car ahead of us. I got out, and while needing to hold onto the post, I called the emergency number. The wind from the other traffic pushed me about significantly. The first thing the operator asked me was, "Where are you?" Unfortunately, the fog had gotten so bad that none of us could read the freeway signs, so I had to just give her the call box number, which was enough thankfully for the police and a tow truck to find us. I went back and sat down in our wind-blown car, and while we were waiting, my husband asked me if I was all right. To my surprise, I said, "Yes, I think so." Then, I asked him if he was all right, and he said, "Yes." We both checked ourselves again, and we were both astonished that we didn't have even the tiniest injury. *We were absolutely fine!*

Even the steering wheel survived my husband's death grip. The police and tow truck eventually found us. I was shocked when the policeman told us that we were very lucky to find a turnout to pull into on this section of the freeway. He said that the one we were in had just been made that week and that there wasn't another turnout for miles. After giving our report to the policeman, he followed us as we slowly limped our car home safely.

The next day, I was thanking the Lord again that we had not hit that concrete barrier. Then I simply asked Jesus, "How is it that we did not hit it? It had been right outside my window; in fact, I could have practically touched it. Jesus, as you know, there wasn't even room for our car to finish its second spin; the barrier was too close. I was also wondering how we started with two spins to the east and then, without hitting the barrier or another car and not turning the wheel, how is that we were suddenly spinning going westward. Our car changed directions by 180 degrees! That just doesn't make sense, Lord, I proclaimed, unless something had stopped our cars' momentum and pushed it the other way." It amazes me sometimes how many questions I toss up at the Lord and then never sit still long enough to hear His answer. This time, however, I did sit still, and suddenly, for a split second, I could see a large angel standing in front of me. He was in my living room, and his right wing was hanging downward as if it was broken. Wow, there was my answer: this angel somehow stopped our car from crashing and then pushed it in the opposite direction. My eyes welled up with tears, and I gave a mighty heartfelt thanks to the Lord and to His angel for protecting us.

Because I was a registered nurse working in a trauma center, I'd seen one too many head injuries from car crashes and knew what it does to the brain. The traumatized brain is usually never the same. This angel saved us and our car, and it also prevented my head from hitting the window. Plus, there was no broken glass that could have injured my eyesight or cut us. And even in the foggy night, God was willing to shed enough light into the dark chaos in front of the other cars so as to miss us. Thank you, Jesus! And thank you for our angel.

We had spun five times, crossed over four lanes of the freeway, hit nothing, and no one else had hit us. Even in thick fog, all the approaching cars were able to slow down enough to miss striking our car. Plus, no one else on the freeway crashed trying to avoid either car as we did our pirouettes on the freeway. Without striking anything, our car suddenly changed directions 180 degrees. So I ask you again, **coincidence or the Hand of God?**

"For he will command his angels concerning you to guard you in all your ways" (Psalm 91:11, NIV). The angel did this for us; he was there and protected us from harm.

"The LORD will keep you from all harm—he will watch over your life; the LORD will watch over your coming and going both now and forevermore" (Psalm 121:7–8, NIV). This scripture seems to cover both east and west directions, even when they are just a split second apart. Thank you, Lord Jesus.

"The angel of the LORD encamps around those who fear him, and he delivers them" (Psalm 34:7, NIV).

"They replied, 'Believe in the Lord Jesus, and you will be saved—you and your household'" (Acts 16:31, NIV). And we were saved in a mighty way; even the other driver was saved. Thank you again, Lord!

THE MIRACLE OF THE SHOOTINGS

I've had miracles happen in my life, but why? Even while I'm writing down the details of my miracles and visions, I still find myself wondering. Can it be true that God wants to use what He has shown me to help others? People who are fighting depression, loneliness, sexual abuse, beatings, neglect, or feelings of worthlessness, I sure hope so. When I started writing this book, I had a vivid memory of the first time I believed that God worked a miracle in my life, and it's one of three gun shooting accidents that I was involved in. I'm embarrassed to say that two of these shooting accidents were my fault, but God granted favor to save my life.

In 1967, my family, whose origin was in Texas, had been big into hunting and fishing. We had rifles and pistols everywhere in our house. One particular night when I was twelve, after my parents' divorce, my mother invited a gentleman over to look at a pistol of hers that wasn't working correctly. The ratchet, a piece of the cylinder in her six-shooter pistol, was worn and didn't turn the cylinder completely. After he had completed examining the gun, I took it and pretended to shoot everything around the house. I'd grown up as a cowgirl, and I played with cap pistols as well as real pistols throughout my childhood. I played with this real gun for an hour or so until my mother took it from me at bedtime.

The next day after school, I invited my neighborhood girlfriend over so that I could show off this pistol to her. She had never even seen a gun up close, and after this day, she probably never wanted to see one again! And you ask why, well…I went into my mother's dresser, where she kept the gun, and I took it out and sat down on the bed next to my friend. At first, I pointed the gun at her stomach, chuckling at her nervousness around a simple little six-shooter. Then I turned the gun and pointed it at my stomach. While I was telling her about the night before, I lifted the pistol to my right temple and started to pull the trigger. At the last fraction of a second, I heard my mother's voice in my head saying, "Don't ever point a gun at anyone!" Just when the hammer started going back, I suddenly pulled the pistol from my head, and wow, to our great surprise, it went off! Holy, holy, holy! I threw the gun on the floor, which could have caused it to fire again, but luckily it did not. Well, my friend didn't stay around very long, and to say the least, she didn't return to my house for a long, long time afterward! She left in such a hurry that I'm not sure she stopped running even when she returned to her house. I'm eternally grateful I had left the front door open, for her sake as well as mine. If the door had been closed, she could have injured herself, and the door, at the speed she was running!

Once I stopped shaking and regained my composure enough to have the ability to walk, I got up to see where the bullet traveled. As I have mentioned before, my legs have a tendency to bounce up and down rapidly when I'm pumped full of adrenaline. The bullet went through the wall into another bedroom. With my legs shaking and feeling like limp noodles, I went to the other bedroom to see the damage that the bullet had done. To my utter surprise, the bullet had missed the television that was up against the wall by an inch or so. Lord, thank you, Jesus! My brain now had a continuous loop playing: my mother is going to kill me over this. I turned around to check the other wall of the bedroom. Through God's grace, the bullet had ricocheted off something in the first wall because its trajectory had gone upward about three feet. Again, thank you, Jesus. The bullet just missed striking my mother's big, four-foot-wide vanity mirror that was over her dresser. My mind was racing; she would have burned me alive if it had hit her mirror. *Well*, I thought, *where had the bullet gone next?*

We had a formal dining room that no one was allowed to enter except at Thanksgiving and Christmas, as the room was filled with antique furniture. I could hear myself saying, *Oh, dear Jesus, no. Not the dining room.* Holding my tears of fright back, I went into the dining room, and there was *no damage* to my absolute amazement. Hallelujah! Nothing! I looked over the entire room three times just to be sure, but I still couldn't understand how it had happened.

I continued to follow the bullet's path and went outside the house. Sure enough, I found the bullet hole. Oh dear God, my neighbor across the street! My legs were working a little better by then, so I sprinted across the street while silently praying, "Lord, please don't let anyone be hurt or worse, dead." Pretending just to be friendly, I knocked on my neighbor's door to see if everyone was okay and hopefully alive. When the wife answered the door, I managed to mumble a friendly "Hi" and proceeded to invite myself into her house. I had to check out their front bedroom because it was the room that was in line with the bullet's trajectory. She offered me a cookie, and when she went to the kitchen to get it, I quickly ducked into her bedroom to scope it out. To my *great joy*, I couldn't see a bullet hole, and everyone was alive. I quickly returned to her living room for the cookie and thanked her most heartily with a quiver in my voice. By the look on her face, my over-eager gratitude must have puzzled her, but I didn't stay around for any questions and quickly ran back home. Again, thank you, Jesus!

Standing in my yard, I could see the bullet hole in the front of my house, along the dining room wall, but how did it get there? I went back into the formal dining room, which shared a common wall with our front porch. I examined both walls over and over, and I finally realized that the bullet had traveled straight down the length of the wall between these two rooms. Again, wow, oh wow!

Luckily, our house had been remodeled and painted before my father divorced my mother. I knew that the leftover paint was probably in the garage. This day I was very glad that my older brother Bill had come home before my mother. For the next hour, he was an angel, helping me patch and paint the holes, thank goodness! I showed him the gun that I had fired, and he pointed out that our mother had two matching six-shooters. After all, she was a hunter and kept guns all over the house. But I had never known about the second, identical six-shooter! Ouch, this was one big lesson for me. I had grabbed the gun that was in her bedroom: the one that, you guessed it, she kept loaded! Evidently, the gun that I had fired was *not* the broken gun that I had played with the night before. Plus, I can promise you that the previously unknown fact that my mother had two identical guns was now seared into my brain, never to be forgotten. My brother and I then had to find the exact bullet to place back in the gun because if it was missing, my mother would have definitely noticed it the next time she picked up the pistol. She was a Texas game hunter at heart and loved to mess with her guns day and night.

We found a replacement bullet for the gun, and by God's grace, she did not notice the wonderful patch jobs to the walls that my brother did that day. Because she was a chain smoker, she couldn't smell that a gun had just been fired in the house. In addition to these miracles, the next day, I noticed sheetrock dust on the top of the television in the second bedroom. Luckily, I was able to quickly wipe it off before my mother could see it. Then I noticed something on the floor, right behind the television. Lo and behold, there was the bullet, all caked with sheetrock dust. I was truly shocked and perplexed: if the bullet ended up here, what had made the holes in the other walls? To this day, I do not know. I was wise enough to wait almost twenty years to tell my mother about the shooting. I ask you, was all of this just a bundle of lucky **coincidences or**

was it the hand of God?

The next shooting accident happened around 1980 when I was in my 20s and staying with my brother, his wife, and their first child, who was about one year old. My brother had caught our mother's gun fever and also had a sizeable collection of pistols and rifles. He shot quite often and was classified as a marksman in the Navy.

One afternoon, he was reloading ammunition and working on his guns in his garage. I didn't have the gun bug, but I had gotten interested in photography and needed some pointers about using my new camera. In all honesty, I must say that a small voice did speak to me as I headed toward his garage. The voice said this was not the time to talk to him about photography or cameras because he was working with guns. But did I listen to it? Heck no. God does speak to me sometimes, in small ways, but as you've read, I had not learned to listen to Him. Patience, being a Fruit of the Spirit, I had not yet acquired. I ignored the warning and walked right into my brothers' garage. He knew more about photography than I did, so I thought that I would drill him for a few answers. After I entered the garage, I pulled up a bench stool so that I could sit right next to him, and I picked up his young son, who was with him, and sat him on my lap. We were elbow-to-elbow so that he could see the camera I was holding and answer my questions. My brother kept working on his pistols, and I kept bothering him with my new camera. After a period of time, I asked him what in the world was he doing. Because I had kept him busy looking at my camera, neither one of us noticed that he had loaded; one of his *two identical* 357 guns/pistols. Of course, this was with a full magnum load! For those that don't know, this is truly a powerful gun. He said he was giving them both hair triggers, which meant that he would have to use very little effort to fire the pistols. To show me what he had done, he pulled the trigger of the pistol in his hand, and it went "click." A split second later, he reached over in front of me, picked up his second 357, and pulled that trigger! Well…holy, holy, holy! *Look who else had two identical pistols, one loaded and one not!*

To this day, I can still see the seven-inch flame that came out of that pistol, probably because it had been only a foot from my face! And I don't know how I "teleported" *so quickly* to the other side of his garage, but I did! I knew for sure that either his baby or me or maybe both of us had been shot. I lifted the baby up despite his excruciating loud screams to examine him, and to my thankful surprise, I couldn't find a single hole in him. I quickly scanned myself, and whew, no hole in me either! I turned to look at my brother; wow. I was shocked to see his normally tanned skin had turned a ghostly white. I almost didn't recognize him. He just stood there for what felt like an eternity, looking at the pistol in his hand, frozen by the fact that he had somehow loaded this second gun, which was obviously unknown to either one of us!

Eventually, he was able to move and came running over to his son and me. He proceeded to give us both an exam because he was also sure that we had been shot. No blood found! His son's red face and shrill screams told us both that he had been frightened to death by that very, very loud gun. To be honest, he wasn't the only one! At first, I thought that it was odd that neither one of us could hear his son's screams very well; he was, obviously, crying his head off. What gives? As it turned out, all three of us were as deaf as a stuffed owl! Consequently, we started screaming at each other just to communicate, which didn't help his son feel any calmer. We eventually got his son to settle down, so we took him to his bedroom to try and get him to take a nap. When we returned to the garage, my brother and I got a sudden urgent need to go check outside, as we could see a relatively large hole in his garage wall. Of course, it also was facing the neighbor's house.

My brother lived in a new housing complex, which meant that his neighbors' house was literally twelve-fifteen feet away. While we were staring at the hole, both our hearts sank: oh God, the neighbor. We ran outside, and because neither one of us could hear very well, we started using a newly invented and unconventional set of hand signs to communicate with each other. We needed to check out his neighbors' house next door for a bullet hole. We leaned as far as we could over his fence and looked and looked until our eyes were getting blurry. What the heck? We were sure the bullet had hit it.

It turned out that the mighty hand of God had intervened again! Apparently, as the bullet exited my brother's garage *somehow*, it just managed to hit a little three-inch metal hinge to the gate on his fence, shattering it into several tiny pieces. What are the odds? I cannot tell you how relieved we both were. We returned to examine the neighbors' house again, and sure enough, we found several small partial bullet holes, but none of them penetrated all the way into their house. Thank you, thank you, Jesus!

You would think we were out of the woods, but we weren't.

His garage needed a fast stucco patch job inside and out before his wife got home. It was strange to think that this time, I was helping him hide the hole before someone got home from work. His wife, also a registered nurse, came home shortly after we finished. It is amazing how quickly you can wipe the snot off a baby's crying face and change his shirt when the mother is coming to see him. We got away with hiding his son's wet shirt, but the child's red face was another problem. His wife was puzzled why the baby had been crying so hard, but we made up some excuse, and she accepted it. We both had to do a lot of extra babysitting the next three days, though, because we didn't want her finding out that the baby was suddenly hard of hearing, too. Yikes! Although she did not notice the patch job, she was thoroughly puzzled why the two of us had been suddenly struck deaf. Our temporary hearing loss was quite apparent at dinner when she had to keep asking over and over for us to pass her the next entree. Our hearing loss, plus the very loud ringing in our heads, lasted a good three days. Oh, joy! Well, you guessed it, I didn't tell her about this little shooting accident until some twenty years later. I waited until after she and my brother were divorced. Again, I thanked the Lord for preventing any fatalities. I ask you: Was it again just, **coincidence or was it the Hand of God?**

Yes, there was yet another shooting accident in 1988 that I was involved in, but this time, it was *not my* fault. This same brother had joined the police reserve, and now he could carry his gun 24/7. Because I was sitting within range of the next accidental shooting, I could have easily been shot. It happened when my brother, his wife, their now eleven-year-old son, about three other people, and I went camping in our local mountains. Yes, my brother had his 357 pistol with him. During the afternoon, his son wanted to play with it, so he took it out of his holster, unloaded it, and handed the gun to his boy. The preteen went around pretending to shoot everything in sight, just like I had done at his age. (*Hmm, I wonder if it is genetic?*) That evening, we all took our chairs to the campfire and sat in a tight circle around it because of the cold weather. The gun holster on my brother's hip was bothering him while he was sitting in his small camping chair, so he pulled the 357 gun out and laid it on a metal table next to him. We were all throwing acorns into the campfire and enjoyed hearing them sizzle, superheat, and then explode. Sometimes the explosions were pretty loud, and we all had to fight the urge to jump out of our chairs as the sound startled us. We were passing drinks around and talking, so none of us noticed that his son had gotten up out of his chair and grabbed (you guessed it) that 357 pistol. Because he was a kid, he didn't think to check whether there were bullets in it either. After all, the gun had been empty just a few hours earlier, so why wouldn't it still be empty? The boy pointed the gun toward the campfire, which happened to be where all of us (oblivious knuckleheads) were seated! And (you guessed it again), he pulled that gun's hair-trigger! I don't know which chair fell over backward first, but mine was in the mix. We all, in unison, screamed out, "What in the Sam Hill was that?" At first, we all assumed that someone had thrown the mother lode of all acorns into the fire. For two to three seconds, no one realized that my brother's gun had been fired, but then we noticed a ghostly white boy crying at the edge of the fire circle, still holding a large 357 pistol (with that hair-trigger, I might add), in his shaking hand. After everyone realized what had happened, we quickly examined each other and were astonished that none of us had been shot. We were so tightly gathered; how had no one been hit? Worse still, because we were in the mountains, if anybody had been shot, we could have never reached town before they would have bled to death. We all gave my brother a good talking to, and after my nephew was reassured everyone was okay, the color of his face returned to normal. With everyone's approval, my brother kept the gun unloaded for the rest of the weekend, and his son didn't play with it anymore, to say the least. We all realized how lucky we had been. I know I said a prayer of thanks. As a little joke between us, any time my brother comes around with a gun, I am now the official bullet counter. He doesn't even argue with me about this annoying ritual.

Three shooting accidents, any of which could have easily been fatal. And I ask you again, was it a **coincidence or the Hand of God** that no one was killed?

How is it that when I turned on my television today, there was a story of an accidental shooting that killed someone? Then I randomly open my Bible to see the following verse: "The LORD will keep you from all harm—he will watch over your life; the LORD will watch over your coming and going both now and forevermore" (Psalm 121:7–8, NIV). Is it a **coincidence or the Hand of God?**

Though I walk in the midst of trouble, you preserve my life. Thank you, Father, for all the protection You have granted my family. It's now the time to acknowledge our sin before God and accept His merciful love for you. Don't turn away. Pray to Jesus for forgiveness and, by faith, receive Jesus Christ into your life. The work of the Holy Spirit in our lives is meant to give us the strength to share with those who need the love, grace, mercy, and forgiveness of Jesus Christ. My heartfelt prayer is that my story has helped those in need. May God bless all who have read this book now and forevermore.

EPILOGUE

"May the God of hope fill you with all joy and peace as you trust in him, so that you may overflow with hope by the power of the Holy Spirit" (Romans 15:13, NIV).

Please remember:

1. if you want to spend eternity in heaven, then know Christ;
2. the Holy Spirit and His angels are with us to help;
3. let go and let God handle it;
4. demonic possession and oppression are real;
5. heaven and hell are real;
6. there is support out there; and
7. God really does love you.

I truly pray that this book has given you encouragement and a new hope that you can live a happier and more fulfilling life. There is help out there under the title "The Bible" and free healing by Jesus Christ. He gives promises of a more abundant life and the gift of protection from the evils in this world. Jesus loves to repair whatever has been destroyed in your life. No matter the depth of your anger, depression, sadness, or hurt, His love for you is so much deeper. "That is what the Scriptures mean when they say, 'No eye has seen, no ear has heard, and no mind has imagined what God has prepared for those who love him'" (1 Corinthians 2:9, NLT).

Nobody is forced to choose eternal separation from God, and nobody suffers this fate by accident. Jesus invites all of us to open the door of our hearts to Him. If we do this, we will enjoy everlasting fellowship with Him. He has sent His angels to care for you, His Holy Spirit to dwell in you, His church to encourage and pray for you, and His word to guide you.

> 'For I know the plans I have for you,' declares the LORD, 'plans to prosper you and not to harm you, plans to give you hope and a future. Then you will call on me and come and pray to me, and I will listen to you. You will seek me and find me when you seek me with all your heart.'
>
> Jeremiah 29:11–13 (NIV)

My prayer is that this book has helped those of you who have had to live under the weight of anger and depression. As a medical professional, I know that depression can be a chemical imbalance in the brain or elsewhere in the body. If this is your diagnosis, I sincerely hope that a doctor can give you the correct medication that will help you. But for those people who have endured hard hits and the downward spiral of depression or in situations where there is a demonic curse, vow, generational sin, or satanic presence in or on you, I pray that this book has given you hope that there is a God out there who wants to help.

In all truthfulness, I know that there is a Holy God and an evil entity called "Satan," both of whom want us. I know there is a war going on for our souls and that the side *we choose* to be on will determine where we spend eternity. You have free will and the right to choose Jesus Christ, Christianity, and salvation in heaven. In heaven, you'll be in your whole and perfectly new healthy body, surrounded by love and a mountain of undeniable joy and happiness. There will be your loved ones and a multitude of glorious angels. And you'll be given a room/home especially prepared for you by our Heavenly Father.

The cross was designed to defeat Satan. If a person does not submit to Jesus, then Satan will control their life. If you do not choose Jesus, by default, you will be with Satan. Satan is the father of lies; with him, you will spend eternity in damnation, in an inferno—fiery pit, unbelievably painful, with loneliness, and indescribable blackness, with no escape possible. God will never force Himself on us, but given the chance, Satan surely will. Your life either sheds light for life and growth, or it casts a shadow for death and destruction. Trust me: there is no middle ground as I once thought. There is only heaven and hell. You get to pick because you have been given free will. You must pick, so please pick wisely.

Jesus is genuine, and He came to earth to suffer as we suffer, to be tempted as we are tempted, and to have the highest demands placed upon Him, more than any human ever could endure. The life Jesus lived was not an easy one. He suffered disgrace, humiliation, shaming, beating, torture, and the pretense of a trial. He was sentenced to the most painful death known at the time. He has first-hand experience in pain, loss, and suffering. He died in our place, taking the judgment we deserve, presenting us flawlessly to His Father in heaven. He is not asking anything of us that He hasn't also experienced. He gave us an instruction book on how to live life on this earth the best way possible. He has a universe of love for each of us. For since the creation of the world, His eternal power and divine nature have been clearly seen so that men are without cause, without excuse. Do not give up on God, instead give up on running from God, for God hasn't given up on you. He wants us to come into fellowship with Him. The Bible shows us a way to spend eternity with Jesus. "Trust in the LORD and lean not on your own understanding; in all your ways submit to him, and he will make your paths straight" (Proverbs 3:5–6, NIV).

John 14:3 (ESV) states: "And if I go and prepare a place for you, I will come again and will take you to myself, that where I am you may be also." *He has gone and personally prepared a room for all of us who will choose to follow Him.* It's a place with no pain, no loss, no want, no hunger, no sickness, no humiliation, and no need. It holds joy, happiness, love, peace, complete health, and marvels untold and inconceivable to man.

For anyone reading this who has *not* given his or her life to Christ, it's not too late. Jesus loves you; He cares for you; and He wants you to come to Him, to lean on Him, and to learn from Him. He wants to have fellowship with you. I pray that you will have the openness to understand the greatness of Christ's love, how wide, how long, how high, and how deep His love is. But the key factor in this scenario is you! He has allowed free will to be ours, to do as we wish.

> For I am convinced that neither death nor life, neither angels nor demons, neither the present nor the future, nor any powers, neither height nor depth, nor anything else in all creation, will be able

to separate us from the love of God that is in Christ Jesus our Lord.

Romans 8:38–39 (NIV)

In closing, I humbly ask our Lord and Savior Jesus Christ to help each of you lay down all sin and pain you may be carrying. It does not matter if your sin and shame were caused by something that you did or if it came upon you by another person, a curse, a vow, or a generational sin; Jesus can heal it. I ask the Lord to lead you to Christian prayer warriors and resources that can help set you free. You will see *that God has placed you here on earth to make a difference for the betterment of mankind. You are no accident!* God has a plan and a purpose for you.

REFERENCES

Chambers, Oswald. *My Utmost for His Highest*. Renewed copyrighted. Ohio: Barbour Publishing, Inc, 1963.

Hampsch, John H. *Healing Your Family Tree*. 2nd ed. Indiana: Our Sunday Visitor, Inc., 1989.

MacNutt, Francis. *Deliverance from Evil Spirits: A Practical Manual*. Michigan: Chosen Books, 1995.

McAll, Kenneth. *Healing the Family Tree*. New ed. London: Sheldon Press, 1986.

Newport, Trevor. *Angeles Demons & Spiritual Warfare*. West Sussex: New Wine Press, 1997.

Smith, Patricia A. *From Generation to Generation: A Manual for Healing*. Florida: Jehovah Rapha Press, 1986.